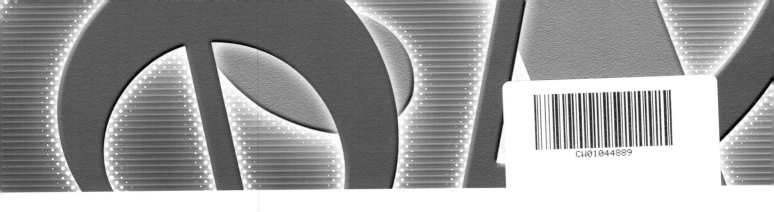

Heinemann
GCSE Music

Mark Phillips

Heinemann Educational Publishers
Halley Court, Jordan Hill, Oxford, OX2 8EJ
Part of Harcourt Education

Heinemann is the registered trademark of
Harcourt Education Limited

Text © Mark Phillips, 2002
First published in 2002

06 05 04 03
9 8 7 6 5 4

British Library Cataloguing in Publication Data
A catalogue record for this book is available from the British Library

ISBN 0 435 81318 8

Designed and typeset by Artistix, Thame, Oxon
Picture research by Debra Weatherley
Printed and bound in Great Britain by Bath Colourbooks

Acknowledgements

Special thanks to Nicola, Benjamin and Henry Phillips for their support and
encouragement with *Heinemann GCSE Music*. Also to Nicola Haisley for constant
and consistent editorial guidance and support.

Thanks to David Motion, Lynsey Brown, colleagues and students at Harlington
Upper School for support and trialing materials, and to Chris Allen, Ian Carfrae,
Mark Horton and James O'Malley for advice and support.

The authors and publishers would like to thank the following for the use of
copyright material: *Infernal Dance* from *The Firebird* by Stravinsky © 1910 P
Juergenson, Moscow © 1933 assigned to B. Schott's Söhne. Reproduced by
permission on pp. 142–6. *No. 23* from *Progressive Studies for Clarinet, Book 1* by
Chris Allen © 1989 by The Associated Board of the Royal Schools of Music.
Reproduced by permission on p. 18. *Reach* Words and music by Todd/Dennis © 19
Music Ltd/BMG Music Publishing Ltd. All Rights Reserved. Used by permission on
pp. 28–30. *Angel* by James MacMillan © 1997 by Boosey & Hawkes Music
Publishers Ltd. Reproduced by permission of Boosey & Hawkes Music Publishers
Ltd on p. 149. *English Folk Song Suite* by Ralph Vaughan Williams © 1924 by
Boosey & Co. Ltd. Reproduced by permission of Boosey & Hawkes Music
Publishers Ltd on pp. 105–6. *Ain't Misbehavin'* Lyrics by Thomas 'Fats' Waller and
Harry Brooks © 1929 by Mills Music Inc and Joy Music Inc. All Rights Reserved.
Reproduction by kind permission of Redwood Music Ltd (Carlin), Iron Bridge
House, 3 Bridge Approach, Chalk Farm, London NW1 8BD on p. 22. *Don't Stop the
Carnival* by Sonny Rollins © 1968 Son Rol Music Company – All Rights Reserved.
Lyrics produced by kind permission of Carlin Music Corp., London NW1 8BD on
pp. 56. *Blue Suede Shoes* by Carl Lee Perkins © 1956 by Hi-Lo Music, Inc. Public
performance rights for USA and Canada controlled by Hi-Lo Music, Inc., a BMI
affiliate. All other rights for the world controlled by Unichappell Music, Inc.
(Rightsong Music, publisher). All Rights Reserved. Carlin Music Corp., London,
NW1 8BD. Lyrics reproduced by kind permission of Carlin Music Corp., London
NW1 8BD on pp. 107–9. *Bamboleo* by Baliardo, Reyes and Bouchikhi. Used by
permission of Chelsea Music on p. 96. *Chasing Sheep is Best Left to Shepherds*
from *The Draughtsman's Contract* by Michael Nyman © 1997 Chester Music
Ltd/Michael Nyman Ltd. All Rights Reserved. International Copyright Secured.
Reproduced by permission on p. 130. *Waltz* from *Five Piano Pieces Op. 23* by
Arnold Schoenberg © 1923 by Edition Wilhelm Hansen A/S, Copenhagen. All
Rights Reserved. International Copyright Secured. Reproduced by permission of
Chester Music Limited on p. 141. *Lightning* from *Songs from Liquid Days* – music
by Philip Glass © 1986 Dunvagen Music Publishers, Inc. All Rights Reserved.
International Copyright Secured. Used by permission of Chester Music Limited on
pp. 147–8. *Three Lions* by Broudie/Baddiel and Skinner. Used by permission of
Chrysalis Music UK on pp. 72–3. *Ever Fallen in Love* by The Buzzcocks.
Reproduced by kind permission of Complete Music Ltd on p. 115. *It's A Sin* Words
and music by Neil Tennant and Christopher Lowe © 1986, Reproduced by
permission of Cage Music Ltd/EMI 10 Music Ltd, London WC2H 0QY on pp. 23–4.
The Mission Music by Ennio Morricone © 1986. Reproduced by permission of EMI
Virgin Music Ltd, London WC2H 0QY on pp. 132–5. *Reach* Words and music by
Cathy Dennis and Andrew Todd © 1999, Reproduced by permission of EMI Music
Publishing Ltd, London WC2H 0QY on pp. 28–30. Theme music from *Psycho
(Prelude)* by B. Herrmann. Used by permission of Hal Leonard Corporation on p. 127.

Re-Rewind the Crowd Say Bo Selecta Words and Music by Mark Hill and Craig
David © 1998 Warner/Chappell Pacific Music Ltd and Windswept Pacific Music Ltd (50%)
Warner/Chappell Music Ltd, London W6 8BS. Reproduced by permission of
International Music Publications Ltd. All Rights Reserved on p. 91. *Twentieth
Century Fox Fanfare* Music by Alfred Newman © 1982 TCF Music Publishing Inc,
USA. Worldwide print rights controlled by Warner Bros. Publications Inc/IMP Ltd.
Reproduced by permission of International Music Publications Ltd. All Rights
Reserved on p. 122. *The Magnificent Seven* Music by Elmer Bernstein © 1960 EMI
Catalogue Partnership, EMI United Partnership Ltd, USA. Worldwide print
controlled by Warner Bros. Publications Inc/IMP Ltd. Reproduced by permission of
International Music Publications Ltd. All Rights Reserved on p. 128. *Lightning*
Words by Suzanne Vegas Music by Philip Glass © 1991 Waifersongs Ltd and
Dunvagen Music Publishers Inc, USA (50%) Warner/Chappell Music Ltd, London
W6 8BS. Reproduced by permission of International Music Publishers Ltd. All
Rights Reserved on p. 147. *The Charleston* Words and music by James Johnson
and Cecil Mack © 1920 Harms Inc, USA. Warner/Chappell Music Ltd, London W6
8BS. Reproduced by permission of International Music Publications Ltd. All Rights
Reserved on p. 86. *Georgy Girl* Words by Jim Dale. Music by Tom Springfield ©
1966 Chappell Music Ltd, London W6 8BS. Reproduced by permission of
International Music Publications Ltd. All Rights Reserved on p. 7–10. *Rock
Around the Clock* by Max Freedman and Jimmy De Knight. Original publication
1954 Myers Music Inc. Edward Kassner Music Co. Limited for the world. Used by
permission. All Rights Reserved on p. 87. *Stayin' Alive* Words and music by Barry
Gibb, Robin Gibb and Maurice Gibb © 1977 Gibb Brothers Music. Used by
permission of Music Sales Ltd. All Rights Reserved. International Copyright
Secured on pp. 89–90. *The Israelites* Words and music by Desmond Dacres and
Leslie Knog © 1969 Florida Music Group Ltd, 8/9 Frith Street, London W1 (25%),
Universal Music Publishing Ltd (75%). Used by permission of Music Sales Ltd. All
Rights Reserved. International Copyright Secured on p. 99. *A Little Respect* Words
and music by Vince Clarke and Andy Bell © 1988 Musical Moments
Limited/Minotaur Music Limited/Sony ATV Music Limited/Sony ATV Music
Publishing (UK) Limited, 10 Great Marlborough Street, London W1F 7LP. Used by
permission of Music Sales Ltd. All Rights Reserved. International Copyright
Secured on pp. 119–21. *Power to All Our Friends* Words and music by Guy
Fletcher and Doug Flett © 1973 Chrysalis Music Limited, The Chrysalis Building,
Bramley Road, London W10. Used by permission of Music Sales Ltd. All Rights
Reserved. International Copyright Secured on p. 20. *All Out of Luck* Words and
music by Selma Bjornsdottir, Sveingorn Baldvinsson and Thorvaldur Bjani ©
Copyright 1999. Universal Music Publishing Ltd. Used by permission of Music
Sales Ltd. All Rights Reserved. International Copyright Secured on p. 23. *Midnight
Train to Georgia* Words and music by Jim Weatherley © 1971 BIBO Music
Publishing, USA. Universal Music Publishing Limited, 77 Fulham Palace Road,
London W6. Used by permission of Music Sales Ltd. All Rights Reserved.
International Copyright Secured on p. 110. *All Right Now* Words and music by
Paul Rodgers and Andy Fraser © 1970 Blue Mountain Music Limited, 8 Kensington
Park Road, London W11. Used by permission of Music Sales Ltd. All Rights
Reserved. International Copyright Secured on p. 112. *Your Song* Words and music
by Elton John and Bernie Taupin © Copyright 1969 Dick James Music Limited.
Universal/Dick James Music Limited, Elsinore House, 77 Fulham Palace Road,
London W6 8JA. Used by permission of Music Sales Ltd. All Rights Reserved.
International Copyright Secured on pp. 116–18. *Crown Imperial* by William Walton
© Oxford University Press 1927. Extracts reproduced by permission on pp. 64–5.
The Voice by Brendan Graham. Used by permission of Brendan Graham and
Peermusic (UK) Ltd on p. 104. *Scale Study for Violin* by Mark Phillips © Mark
Phillips on p. 18. *St Thomas* by Sonny Rollins. Used by permission of Prestige
Music Ltd on p. 57. *Little Piano Piece No. 6, Op. 19* by Arnold Schoenberg ©
1913, 1940 by Universal Edition A.G., Wien/UE 5069 on p. 139. *Rewind* by
David/Hill. Used by permission of Windswept Music on p. 91.

The publishers would like to thank the following for permission to use
photographs: AKG Photo/Vienna, Histor. Museum der Stadt Wien on p. 81;
Bridgeman Art Library/Guildhall Art Gallery, corporation of London, UK (Queen
Caroline) on p. 61; Bridgeman Art Library/Scottish National Portrait Gallery,
Edinburgh (George I) on p. 61; The British Library on p. 84; Corbis on pp. 88 and
73; Ninder Johal on p. 94; The Kobal Collection on pp. 9 and 126; The Movie
Store Collection on p. 124; Mark Phillips on p. 16; Pictorial Press/Jeffery Moyer
on p. 116; Pictorial Press/Sunstills on p. 22; Redferns/Dave Peabody on p. 103;
Redferns/Nicky J. Sims on p. 28; Retna/Adrian Boot on p. 115; Retna UK/Ian Yates
on p. 94; Rex Features/Richard Young on p. 102; United States Virgin Islands
Division of Tourism on p. 57; Zach productions on p. 66.

Websites

Links to appropriate websites are given throughout the book/pack. Although these
were up to date at the time of writing, it is essential for teachers to preview these
sites before using them with pupils. This will ensure that the web address (URL) is
still accurate and the content is suitable for your needs.

We suggest that you bookmark useful sites and consider enabling pupils to access
them through the school intranet. We are bringing this to your attention as we are
aware of legitimate sites being appropriated illegally by people wanting to
distribute unsuitable or offensive material. We strongly advise you to purchase
suitable screening software so that pupils are protected from unsuitable sites and
their material.

If you do find that the links given no longer work, or the content is unsuitable,
please let us know. Details of changes will be posted on our website.

Tel: 01865 888058   www.heinemann.co.uk

CONTENTS

INTRODUCTION
All about Heinemann GCSE Music

Whichever one of the three GCSE music specifications you are studying – AQA, Edexcel or OCR – you will be studying four or five different Areas of Study. Within each Area of Study, you will be engaged in listening, composing and performing tasks that are related to the central theme of the Area of Study. For example, if you are an AQA student, you will study *Music for film*. Your work could include listening to and analysing the soundtracks for a variety of films, performing excerpts from those soundtracks and composing your own film music. If you are an Edexcel student, you will study *The popular song in context*. Your work could include listening to and analysing a wide variety of pop songs and styles from the 1950s onwards, performing some of those songs and composing songs of your own. If you are an OCR student, you will study *Dance music*. Your work could include listening to nineteenth-century waltzes and disco music from the 1970s, performing some of the music and composing some dance music of your own.

Heinemann GCSE Music contains ten projects. Each project has a strong link to at least one of the GCSE Areas of Study, with individual listening, composing and performing units within the project having links to other Areas of Study. On pages v–vi, you will see grids that gives an overall view of where you can find material that will help you for your particular Areas of Study. As you can see, whichever of the three courses you are studying, you will find every part of *Heinemann GCSE Music* of use.

In this student book, you will find a comprehensive selection of music to listen to (recordings of the pieces are provided on the double audio CD that accompanies *Heinemann GCSE Music*) and explanations of key terms and phrases that are used in the analyses of the pieces. There are composition tasks for you to attempt and ideas for giving performances of the pieces that you have listened to.

In the teacher's resource file, there are additional composition, performance and listening tasks for you to try, together with useful resources, such as fuller scores for you to follow as you listen.

A final feature of the teacher's resource file is the 'Key words and terms' grid that is provided for each project. These grids list many of the key words and terms that you will need to know for your final listening examination. Your teacher will give you copies of the grids at various points during your GCSE music course. The idea is for you to write in your own definition of each of these words and terms as they are covered in your lesson. Do not worry about trying to write a precise dictionary style definition for each word or term to start with. It is much better for your understanding for you to define the word or term in your own words and style, although it would be sensible for you to confirm your definition with a published music dictionary after the lesson.

Whilst on the subject of working after lessons, for each project there are six extension tasks provided that you might like to try in your own time. Alternatively, your teacher might like to set them for homework.

There is one final resource that is absolutely essential for your success at GCSE music – your teacher! He or she is the person who should plan your work schedule, set your deadlines, make sure that all the necessary examination administration takes place and do everything to help aim for your highest possible grade in the final examination. He or she should use *Heinemann GCSE Music* creatively to help give you the best possible skills and experiences and should make sure that you have access to as much music and music-making as possible. Make good use of the expertise and resources that your teacher provides; make good use of all the resources in *Heinemann GCSE Music*; and above all, enjoy every minute of your GCSE music course!

AQA specification

Area of Study	Central Heinemann GCSE Music project(s)	You will find these projects particularly useful as well:									
		Forms and structures	Using instruments and voices	Developing melodies	Western art music styles	Music for special occasions	Dance music	World music and fusions	Popular music styles and cultures	Music for film	Art music of the twentieth century
Music for film	Music for film	✓	✓		✓	✓	✓			★	✓
Music for dance	Dance music/ Popular music styles and cultures	✓		✓	✓	✓	★	✓	★		✓
Music for special events	Music for special occasions	✓			✓	★		✓		✓	✓
Orchestral landmarks	Western art music styles	✓	✓	✓	★	✓	✓	✓		✓	✓
The popular song since 1960	Popular music styles and culture	✓	✓	✓		✓	✓	✓	★	✓	

OCR specification

Area of Study	Central Heinemann GCSE Music project(s)	You will find these projects particularly useful as well:									
		Forms and structures	Using instruments and voices	Developing melodies	Western art music styles	Music for special occasions	Dance music	World music and fusions	Popular music styles and cultures	Music for film	Art music of the twentieth century
Exploiting the resource	Using instruments and voices/Western art music styles	✓	★	✓	★	✓	✓	✓	✓	✓	✓
Techniques of melodic composition	Developing melodies	✓	✓	★	✓	✓	✓	✓	✓	✓	✓
Dance music	Dance music/ Popular music styles and cultures	✓		✓	✓	✓	★	✓	★		✓
Traditions and innovations	World music and fusions					✓	✓	★	✓	✓	✓

Edexcel specification

Area of Study	Central Heinemann GCSE Music project(s)	You will find these projects particularly useful as well:									
		Forms and structures	Using instruments and voices	Developing melodies	Western art music styles	Music for special occasions	Dance music	World music and fusions	Popular music styles and cultures	Music for film	Art music of the twentieth century
Repetition and contrast in western Classical music, 1600–1899	Forms and structures/Western art music styles ↵	★	✓	✓	★	✓	✓			✓	
New directions in western Classical music, 1900–present day	Art music of the twentieth century					✓		✓		✓	★
The popular song in context	Popular music styles and cultures	✓	✓	✓		✓	✓	✓	★		
Rhythms, scales and modes in music from around the world	World music and fusions					✓	✓	★	✓	✓	

PRELUDE FROM TE DEUM
Charpentier (1643–1704)

Music for an occasion

If you have ever watched the Eurovision Song Contest you will probably have heard this piece of music that opens the show every year. The music, in stark contrast to the songs that follow it, is by the French Baroque composer Marc-Antoine Charpentier. The piece was originally composed as the prelude, or introductory piece, to Charpentier's *Te Deum* for choir and orchestra.

Charpentier composed his *Prelude* for orchestra, including trumpets and timpani. A recording is on CD 1, track 1. The recorded performance is in D major, the score given here is in the key of C major.

The piece is in **rondo form** – AABACAA. As you listen to the recording, trace through the section and notice how the main A idea keeps on returning.

Performance tasks

◆ In groups of between two and four, give your own performance of this piece. The score that is given here is for a melody instrument and accompaniment, so it would be possible to perform with just two of you. However, you will notice that the bass line of the accompaniment can be taken separately as a single line for a bass guitar, cello,

trombone, or other bass instrument. For other instruments, you may have to trace through the treble clef line of the accompaniment and draw out your own instrumental part. Try to make your lines as smooth but as interesting as possible.

◆ Write out your individual parts on manuscript paper and remember to transpose the parts if necessary.

PERFECT AND IMPERFECT CADENCES

The language of music

It is often said that music is the universal language. Certainly, music is an extremely expressive means of communication and later in this book we will explore ways in which music can communicate a variety of different messages.

Like all verbal languages (languages that are written and spoken) music consists of a number of important elements. In English, French and German, for example, the language is formed and structured from individual letters or letter sounds, which are then combined to form words, which are then put together to form sentences. These sentences are organized to make sense through the use of punctuation.

Cadences

In music, the letter sounds are individual notes. These notes are put together to form small motifs and these motifs join to make phrases. We can give these melodic phrases musical punctuation by adding short, two-chord harmonic progressions at key points in the phrase. These musical punctuation marks are called **cadences**.

The perfect cadence

In the English language, we mark the end of a sentence with a full stop. In music, the end of a phrase is marked by a **perfect cadence**. A perfect cadence is formed by chord V immediately followed by chord I.

The imperfect cadence

The title **imperfect cadence** suggests the opposite of a perfect cadence – chord I followed by chord V.

Sometimes an imperfect cadence can take the form of chord IV followed by chord V, or chord II followed by chord V.

Analysis tasks

◆ Look at the end of section A of Charpentier's *Prelude* below. Where does a perfect cadence come?
◆ A perfect cadence ends with chord I. Why does this cadence help bring the phrase to a 'full stop'?

◆ Whereabouts in section A of Charpentier's *Prelude* can you find an imperfect cadence?

MODULATION

Key information

When you look at the score and play the opening bars of Charpentier's *Prelude*, you can quickly tell that the piece is in the key of C major. The key signature after the clef at the start of each stave contains no sharps or flats; the music sounds major and the harmony of the first three bars strongly emphasizes the tonic and dominant chords (C and G) in C major.

Changing key

However, the music does not stay in the key of C major for the whole piece. At various points the music changes into other keys. When this happens we say that the music has **modulated** from the tonic key.

When music modulates from a tonic key it will most likely change to another closely related key. By this we mean a key that has a key signature similar to that of the tonic key, or a key that has another element in common with the tonic key.

Closely related keys to C major

C major has no sharps or flats in its key signature, so the keys of F major (with one flat in the key signature) and G major (with one sharp in the key signature) are closely related to the key of C major. If you wanted to modulate from C major to F major, you would only need to change one note – B to B flat. Similarly, if you wanted to change from C major to G major, you would only have to change one note – F to F sharp.

The key of A minor is also closely related to C major. A minor has no sharps or flats in the key signature, but it does have one note that is regularly sharpened (in both harmonic and melodic versions of the scale) – the leading note G sharp. To modulate from C major to A minor, you would only have to change one note – G to G sharp.

Drawing up a key grid

You can chart the closely related keys in a piece of music by drawing up a 'key grid'.

	TONIC KEY	
(0 sharps, 1 flat) **F major**	(0 sharps, 0 flats) **C major**	(1 sharp, 0 flats) **G major**
(0 sharps, 1 flat plus C sharp) **D minor**	(0 sharps, 0 flats plus G sharp) **A minor**	(1 sharp, 0 flats plus D sharp) **E minor**

Modulations in Charpentier's *Prelude*

Now go back to the score of Charpentier's *Prelude* on pages 1–3. As you know, this piece is in rondo form.

The first A section is from bars 1–8. This section is completely in the key of C major. Whenever the A section is repeated, from bars 9–16, bars 25–32 and bars 41–56, this is always the case. The A sections never modulate from the key of C major.

However, one of the things that makes the B and C sections different from the A section is that in these sections the music does modulate away from the tonic key.

In the B section, the music modulates firstly to A minor (bars 19–20) and then to G major (bars 22–4).

In the C section, the modulations are even more adventurous and fast moving. The music modulates from C major to A minor (bar 36), and then to A *major* (bar 37), D major (bar 38) and G major (bar 39), before returning to C major for the final A section.

Analysis task

◆ Listen to the recording of Charpentier's *Prelude*. How does he differentiate between sections A, B and C apart from the differences caused by the modulations?

If you place all the major or all the minor key signatures in a logical order, from C major (no sharps) to G major (1 sharp), and so on, you will notice two things. Firstly, the consecutive keys are an interval of a perfect fifth apart. Secondly, eventually you will arrive back to C major. We call this logical order the **circle of fifths**. This diagram shows how the circle of fifths works and is a good aid to help you remember key signatures and relative major/minor keys.

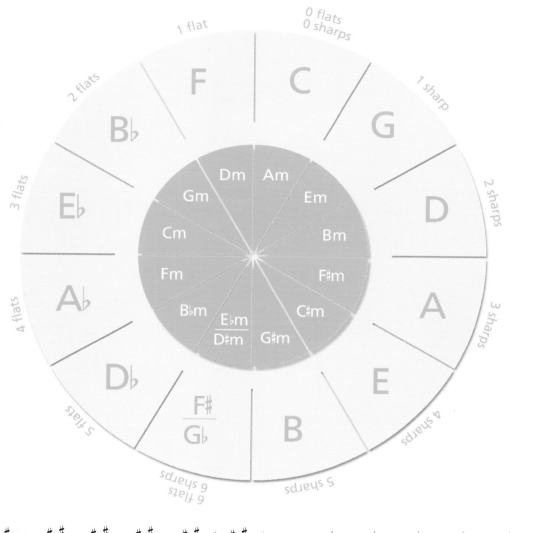

GEORGY GIRL

Tom Springfield and Jim Dale

Listen to this song on CD 1, track 2.

*Hey there! Georgy Girl! Dreaming of the
someone you could be.
Life is a reality, you can't always run away.*

*Don't be so scared of changing and re-
arranging yourself.
It's time for jumping down from the shelf –
a little bit.*

*Hey there! Georgy Girl! There's another
Georgy deep inside,
Bring out all the love you hide and oh,
what a change there'd be,
The world would see a new Georgy Girl.*

About this song

This song was a hit in 1967 for The Seekers.

The song was composed by Tom Springfield (brother of singer Dusty Springfield) with lyrics by Jim Dale (who is probably better known for his roles in the *Carry On* films). *Georgy Girl* was in fact written as the title track for the film of the same name. The film was released in 1966 and featured the story of a young girl (played by Lynn Redgrave) growing up in London during the 'swinging sixties'.

Performance task

◆ The vocal arrangement given here is in two parts, in the key of C major. You will notice that the vocal range for the upper part is quite large, ranging from G below middle C to D, an octave-and-a-half higher. The lower part only has a range of an octave, from C to C.
◆ Perform this song in small groups, with at least one singer per vocal part and an accompanying instrument. The teacher's resource file also gives the guitar chord symbols should you need them. There is also a catchy, bouncy instrumental introduction that would go well on a flute or violin.

Ternary form

The song *Georgy Girl* is structured into what is known as **ternary form**. The term 'ternary' implies that the form should have three sections arranged into A–B–A pattern. However, in some cases, pieces in ternary form, or 'standard form', as it is known in popular music, have four sections – A–A–B–A, with the first A section repeated at the start. These sections are most usually defined by melodic content and by the use of different tunes to show different sections. If you follow through the score of *Georgy Girl* on pages 7–8, you should see the ternary form take shape.

As you can see, the form is well balanced. All of the sections are eight bars long, except for the last section, which is extended to eleven bars. In popular music, the B section is sometimes known as the 'middle eight' section.

Note that the three A sections are marked A, A1 and A2. This is because, although they are all largely the same and share melodic material, they do have slight differences. Can you spot the differences between A, A1 and A2?

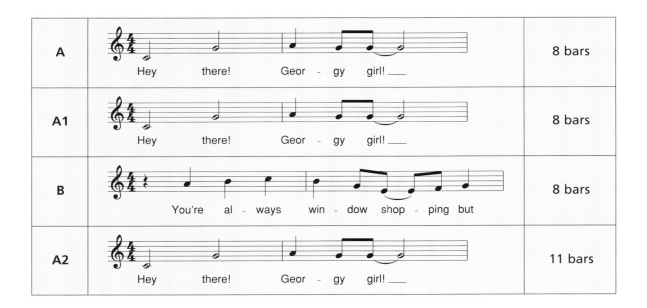

Interrupted cadences

As we have seen, the final section of this song is longer than the previous three sections. This extension is created through the use of an interrupted cadence. This form of musical punctuation is much like a semi-colon in written verbal language – it marks a resting place in the phrase, but not **the** final resting place. In terms of chords, an interrupted cadence usually features chord V followed by chord VI.

Look at the last line of *Georgy Girl* below. Can you see where the interrupted cadence provides a musical 'semi-colon' before the phrase is finally brought to a conclusion? (Remember that this arrangement is in the key of C major and that chord V will be the chord of G, with chord VI being the chord of A minor.)

GAVOTTE FROM ORCHESTRAL SUITE NO. 1 IN C MAJOR

J.S. Bach (1685–1750)

The **gavotte** was an old dance that originated in the courts of France. It was a formal, stately dance with four beats to the bar. A particular musical characteristic of the gavotte was the two beat anacrusis (lead-in) that started each phrase.

This **gavotte** was composed by J.S. Bach as part of his first suite of dances for orchestra. Listen to the recording of this piece, on CD 1, track 3, and follow through the score as you listen. The top line of each system is the melody line, which you may find easier to concentrate on the first time you listen to the piece. After that, you might like to follow one of the other lines to gain a different perspective of the piece.

Performance tasks

◆ In groups of at least four, make your own arrangement and performance of Bach's *Gavotte*.

◆ All of the parts given on the score above are in the key of C. If you are playing an instrument in B flat, such as the clarinet, you will need to transpose your part – unless all instruments in the group are B flat instruments.

◆ Remember that the third line is in the alto clef and may also have to be re-written, and the fourth line is in the bass clef.

◆ Although this piece is in the key of C major, the music does modulate to other keys. Be careful with the accidentals.

Binary form

Bach's *Gavotte* is structured into what is known as **binary form**. As the term 'binary' implies, the music is structured into two sections – A–B.

When we analysed *Georgy Girl*, we saw that the ternary form was defined by the use of different melodic themes to show different sections of the form. In Bach's binary form, the two different sections are defined not by melody but by **key**.

The first section of the *Gavotte* is eight bars long. The section starts in the tonic key of C major:

By the end of this section, it has modulated to the dominant key of G major:

The second half starts with the chord of G major, but quickly moves off into other keys, such as D minor, A minor and F major. Finally, the music arrives back in the tonic key of C major, just in time for the final cadence of section B:

This illustration shows the binary form of Bach's *Gavotte* more clearly:

Section A	Section B
C → → → → G	G → Dm → Am → F → C

Analysis tasks

◆ Refer back to the key grid that was used when analysing Charpentier's *Prelude* (on pages 1–3). This key grid can also be used for Bach's *Gavotte*, as both pieces are written in C major.

◆ Go through the score on pages 11–12 and spot exactly where each modulation occurs.

◆ Which closely related key (to C major) does Bach *not* modulate to in his *Gavotte*?

◆ This piece is in binary form, a form defined by changes of key. The piece is also **monothematic**. What does the term 'monothematic' mean? What evidence is there to prove that this piece is monothematic?

Sonata form

We have seen how binary form was defined and structured by keys and modulations. Bach worked during the Baroque period of musical style. Towards the end of this period composers composed more extensive binary form movements, with the B sections modulating to more distant keys for longer periods of time. Also, the modulation to the dominant key that came at the end of the A section in binary form came earlier in the A section and lasted longer. To prevent these longer movements from becoming tedious, composers introduced a new melodic idea into the dominant key part of the A section, rather than having a single

melodic idea throughout the movement. At the end of the B section, there was a much longer section back in the tonic key. Here, composers often presented all of the melodic material first heard in the A section, but with everything in the tonic key.

These pieces were often composed for solo instruments with keyboard accompaniment, or keyboard alone, and they became known as **sonatas** – literally pieces to be sounded or played. This expanded form was known as **sonata form**.

Think back to the analysis of Bach's *Gavotte* and the analysis table that showed the binary form of the movement:

Section **A**	Section **B**
C ——→ G	G → Dm → Am → F → C
Tonic key ——→ dominant key	Modulating through other keys → tonic key

In the sonata form, the A section is called the **exposition**, where the listener is exposed to the tonic and dominant keys. The B section is called the **development**, where the keys are developed away from the tonic and the dominant to other keys. Finally, when the tonic key returns at the end of the piece, it is called the **recapitulation**, recapping what has been heard at the start of the piece.

An analysis table for sonata form looks like this:

Exposition	Tonic	This section is based in the tonic (main key) of the piece. The main melody on which this section is based is sometimes called the **first subject**.
	Dominant	This section is based in the dominant key of the piece. This section is sometimes based on a new melody, which is sometimes called the **second subject**.
Development	Other keys	In this section, the music modulates to keys other than the tonic and dominant. When you analyse a movement in sonata form, have your 'key grid' handy.
Recapitulation	Tonic	This section is based in the tonic (main key) of the piece. The main melody on which this section is based is sometimes called the **first subject**.
	Tonic	This section is also based in the tonic key (when it came in the exposition it was in the dominant). The second subject melody will be transposed into the tonic key for this section.

SYMPHONY NO. 29, K201, 1ST MOVEMENT
Mozart (1756–91)

As with all musical theory, it is much easier to understand sonata form when you see and hear it working in practice. This symphony, in the key of A major, was composed by Wolfgang Amadeus Mozart in early 1774, when he was only eighteen years old. If you think that is impressive, remember that this was his twenty-ninth symphony and something like the 200th of his catalogued compositions. The 'K' number found after each of Mozart's works refers to Ludwig Ritter Von Köchel who catalogued all of Mozart's known works in the nineteenth century.

Listen to the recording of this movement on CD 1, track 4, and as you listen, follow the analysis table below. You will see that the movement follows the sonata form structure. To help you even more as you listen, a few bars of the score for each section is given.

Exposition
Tonic
Based in the tonic (main key) of the piece. The main melody is sometimes called the **first subject**.

Dominant
Based in the dominant key of the piece, but sometimes based on a new melody, which is sometimes called the **second subject**.

Development
Other keys
The music modulates to keys other than the tonic and dominant.

Recapitulation
Tonic
Based in the tonic (main key) of the piece. The main melody is sometimes called the **first subject**.

Tonic
Based in the tonic key (in the exposition it was in the dominant). Here, the second subject melody will be transposed into the tonic key.

During your GCSE music course, you will have to produce at least two of your own original compositions. The subject or theme of your composition will depend upon the specification that you are studying towards, the Area of Study that you are working in and the way that your teachers have organized your course.

When you come to work on your own compositions, it is quite probable that you will choose to work on an instrument with which you have technical competence and confidence. If you choose to compose for an instrument that you do not play yourself, then you start with the disadvantage that you do not know *from your own performing experience* what is easy, difficult or possible on that instrument. If you do choose to compose for an instrument that you are not familiar with, you will need to do some extra research about the challenges and potential of that instrument.

When you set out to compose music to be played on your own instrument, or when you need to plan composing for another instrument, there are a number of key issues that you should address (see opposite). Planning ahead will save time in the long run and should ensure that your music does not just work well as a piece of music, but that it also works well in performance for the instrument(s) that it is written for.

◆ What is the natural range of the instrument(s)? Am I/is the performer able to play across the full potential range of the instrument?

◆ What is your/your performer's standard of performance? For example, if your performer has just passed his or her Grade 4 exam, what are the technical standards and expectations for a player at that grade? You might then like to stretch your performer by writing music at just *beyond* that standard.

◆ Do notes in the different registers of the instrument's range have different sound qualities? For example, the highest notes of the flute have a shrill, piercing quality, whilst the lower notes have a much more mellow sound and do not project as well.

◆ Are there particular keys that are easier to play than others?

◆ Are there particular types of interval or pattern that are easy/difficult to play on this instrument? For example, on the double-bass, tonic-fifth-octave leaps fall easily under the hand and are easy to play. This is particularly useful when writing tonic-dominant harmonies in root position.

◆ Are there any special playing techniques that could be exploited, such as harmonics and pizzicato for strings, flutter-tonguing on flutes and so on?

◆ Look at examples of good writing for your chosen instrument(s). Your GCSE music teacher or, more likely, your instrumental teacher will be able to help you with this.

Finally, remember that throughout the history of music, successful composers have never been afraid to ask advice from performers about what is and is not possible on an instrument.

By way of example, take a look at the two pieces that follow on pages 17 and 18. The pieces have been composed for a woodwind instrument and a string instrument and both exploit particular performance techniques on the chosen instrument.

STUDY FOR CLARINET NO. 23
Chris Allen

If you have taken an Associated Board grade exam on the clarinet, you may well have learnt to play a study by Chris Allen. Chris has composed two sets of clarinet studies for the Associated Board. As well as being a composer, he also works as a peripatetic clarinet teacher and each of his studies was composed with a specific teaching and learning technique in mind.

Below is *Study No. 23* from his first book, which is on CD 1, track 5 and performed by Chris Allen himself. Chris Allen says of this study:

When I composed this study, I had two aims in mind. Firstly, I wanted students to use the music to help them achieve a good legato sound whilst crossing over some fairly wide intervals. This could be particularly tricky when approaching A naturals and B flats from below. Secondly, I wanted to produce a piece of music for unaccompanied solo clarinet, which, nonetheless, contained both 'melody' and 'accompaniment'. In the opening two bars, for example, the repeated Gs are accompanying notes (like a drone), whilst the other notes form a smooth melodic line. The challenge to the student is to bring out a legato melody whilst keeping the accompanying note in a supporting role.

Performance tasks

◆ If you are a clarinettist, try performing the study yourself. How well can you meet the challenges set in the piece?

◆ If you play another instrument, what amendments would you have to make to the piece in order to make it playable on your instrument? Does the piece present you with the same challenges that Chris Allen has specified for the clarinet, or does the piece present different challenges for your instrument?

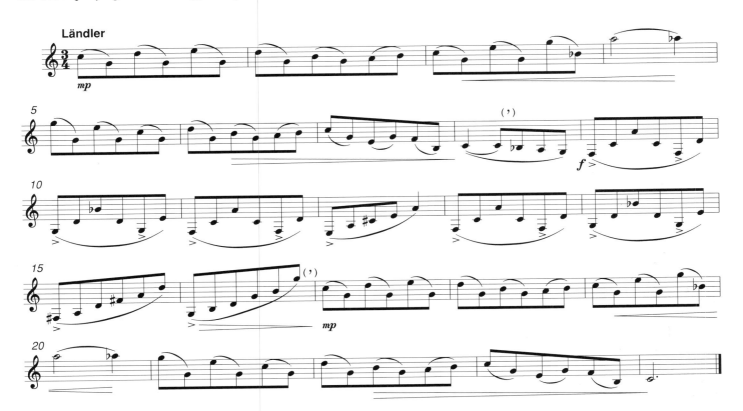

SCALE STUDY FOR VIOLIN
Mark Phillips

When you have analysed (and maybe even played) the clarinet study by Chris Allen, take a look at this study, which was composed for a young violinist.

A recording of it can be found on CD 1, track 6, played by the violinist Ian Smith.

Analysis tasks

- Apart from the scale of C major, what are the other scales that are 'tested' in this study?
- What are the other challenges that are presented to the young string player in this study?

- Could this study be useful to help players of other instruments who are learning to play scales? If so, what amendments would you have to make to the score?

USING THE VOICE
Setting words to music

At some stage in your GCSE composition work, you are going to be faced with the challenge of setting some words to music. Like any instrument, it is important to understand the human voice if you are to make maximum use of its potential in your compositions. It is also important to know about the techniques that can be used in setting words to music.

Know your strengths

When you have been given, have chosen or have written words to be set to music, spend some time reading through the words and deciding where the natural stresses of the words fall. Here is an example, with naturally (spoken) stressed syllables underlined.

> Listen to the <u>pour</u>ing rain
> <u>Beat</u>ing on the <u>roof</u> again.

When you come to set these words to music, you could match these naturally spoken accents with the accent beats in a bar. For example:

If you added pitch to this rhythm, you might come up with the following idea:

Syllabic word setting

You will notice that there is exactly one note to every syllable of the text. This is called **syllabic word setting**.

Melismatic word setting

If you wanted to make your word setting a little more colourful or even downright showy, you could write more than one note to each syllable, with each syllable of the words stretching over a number of notes.

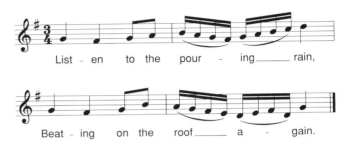

Where a syllable is given more than one note, the music/word setting is referred to as being **melismatic**.

Antecedent and consequent

In the short example used on this page, you will have noticed that the two lines set to music are similar in several ways:

◆ The lines rhyme poetically – 'rain' rhymes with 'again'.
◆ Each line contains seven syllables.

The form of the words can play an important part in shaping the form of the music that the same words are set to.

◆ As the two lines are of the same length, it follows that, when each line is turned into a musical phrase, each phrase should be of the same length.
◆ As the number of syllables in each line (and the natural rhythm/stresses of the words) are the same, it follows that the two lines could have similarly matched rhythms and melodies.

Look at the syllabic and melismatic settings on this page and you will see this in practice. You will also notice that the two phrases form a sort of 'question and answer' idea – the first phrase ends with an ascending pattern after starting in the same way as the first phrase.

These two phrases are referred to as the **antecedent** (question) and **consequent** (answer) phrase.

Listen carefully to the opening of this song, which is on
CD 1, track 7. Follow this vocal score as you listen.

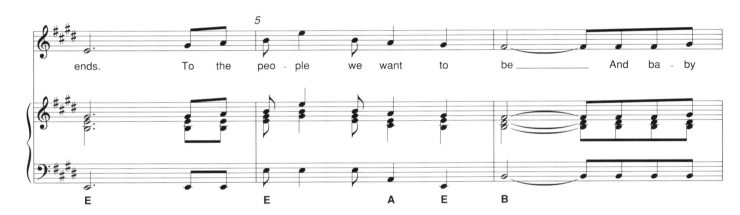

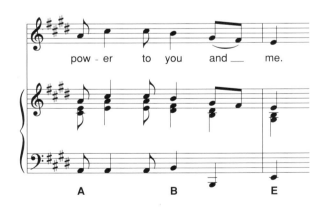

Analysis tasks

◆ Is the word setting in this extract syllabic or melismatic?
◆ Is this extract sung in unison or in harmony?
◆ The whole of the extract printed above is sung *a cappella*. What does *a cappella* mean?
◆ What happens immediately after the printed extract?
◆ Look carefully at the chords used in this extract. What do you notice?

Performance task

◆ A fuller score of this extract is provided in the teacher's resource file. Listen to the recording of Cliff Richard performing this song and then make your own arrangement of the song. You should make a special effort to perform an *a cappella* four-part harmony version of the opening section.

QUEEN OF THE NIGHT'S ARIA FROM THE MAGIC FLUTE

Mozart

- Listen to CD 1, track 8.
- Is the word setting syllabic or melismatic?

- How does the accompaniment (orchestral writing) change after the words 'so sei sie dann...'? Why do you think Mozart makes this change?
- What does this aria say about the character of the Queen of the Night? What is it about the music that she sings that leads you to this opinion?

SCAT'S JAZZ!

In *Power to All Our Friends* and *The Queen of the Night's Aria*, we heard two very different, but equally distinctive, singing styles. In both cases, the vocal music was set to words. In the case of *Power to All Our Friends*, the word setting was syllabic, and in the case of the Mozart aria, the word setting was largely melismatic.

Vocal music does not always have to be set to words, however. A number of composers have included 'wordless voices' as part of an orchestral sound to great effect. One of the most well-known examples of this is in *The Planets* by Gustav Holst.

In jazz and pop music, singers often perform in a style known as **scat**. In this style, the singer vocalizes – uses the voice as if it were an instrument – or sings to abstract vowel sounds or nonsense words like 'doo bee doo bee doo'. You will be able to think of countless examples of singers doing this!

This is not the total of what scat singing is about, though. Many jazz singers use a wide range of singing techniques to create different vocal timbres in the same way that an instrumentalist would get different timbral qualities from using vibrato or a mute.

Listen to the recording of Louis Armstrong performing Fats Waller's famous song *Ain't Misbehavin'*, which is on CD 1, track 9.

> *No-one to talk with, all by myself,*
> *No-one to walk with but I'm happy on the shelf.*
> *Ain't misbehavin', I'm savin' my love for you.*
>
> *I know for certain the one I love,*
> *I'm throu' with flirtin', it's just you I'm thinkin' of,*
> *Ain't misbehavin', I'm savin' my love for you.*
>
> *Like Jack Horner in the corner,*
> *Don't go nowhere. What do I care?*
> *Your kisses are worth waitin' for, believe me.*
>
> *I don't stay out late, don't care to go.*
> *I'm home about eight, just me and my radio.*
> *Ain't misbehavin', I'm savin' my love for you.*

At the start of the extract, you will hear a traditional Dixieland jazz band playing – piano, drums and bass providing the rhythm, with trumpet, trombone and clarinet as the 'front-line' instruments. Louis Armstrong himself is playing the trumpet. After the instruments have played through the chorus structure once, Louis Armstrong sings the chorus.

Listening tasks

◆ In the opening instrumental section, which instrument plays the melody?

◆ What functions do the other two 'front-line' instruments have in this opening section?

◆ When Louis Armstrong sings, where does he sing in a 'scat' style?

◆ Why do you think he saves the scat singing for these moments?

◆ One of the characteristics of Louis Armstrong's singing style is 'growling'. How would you describe this singing style and where and when does he use this style?

◆ Do you notice any similarities between Louis Armstrong's singing style and the way that he plays the trumpet?

Setting words to music

On page 19, we explored strategies to use when setting words to music. Remember that it is important to:

◆ give consideration to where the natural stresses and accents of the words fall

◆ decide whether your words require a syllabic setting (one note per syllable) or a melismatic setting (several notes per syllable).

◆ balance musical phrases by using antecedent and consequent phrases.

Writing a strong melody really is a craft and there are techniques that you can learn that will help you compose strong melodies. As the old saying goes, 'You can't beat a good tune', so here is how to compose one.

Start with a motif

A **motif** is a short fragment of melody that forms the core of the melody. Most tunes start with a short motif that the composer then develops, manipulates and expands into a fully developed melodic phrase.

There are a number of methods that composers use to transform motifs into melodies. The simplest is **repetition**.

Repeating your motif

In their song *All Out of Luck* on CD 1, track 10, the composers, Selma Björnsdóttir, Sveinbjörn I Baldvinsson and Thorvaldur Bjarni Thorvaldsson, start by stating a simple two bar motif:

To expand this motif into a longer eight bar melody, the composers simply repeat this motif three times. By the third time, the music could become a little boring so the composers extend the motif by adding two extra bars to the 'tail' of the motif:

The techniques used by the composers in this example are repetition and **extension**.

Moving by step

Another method of motif repetition is **sequence**, where the composer repeats the motif, but instead of repeating it at exactly the same pitch, repeats it up or down a step. For example, in the song *It's a Sin* by Neil Tennant and Chris Lowe (The Pet Shop Boys), on CD 1, track 11, another simple two bar motif is used:

To make a longer melody, this motif is also played three times. The second playing of the motif starts down a step from the previous playing of the motif, in sequence, and, like the example from *All Out of Luck*, on the third playing of the motif, the composers use a variation to prevent the music from becoming too repetitive.

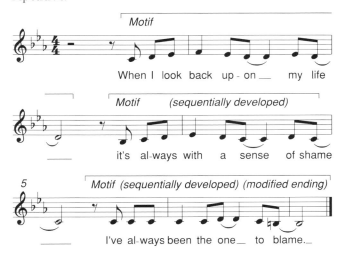

The techniques used by the composers in this example are **sequential repetition** and **extension**.

Expanding and contracting

In the last movement of his *Sinfonia Concertante, K297b*, Mozart uses a simple one bar motif to construct his melody:

Listen to CD 1, track 12. Mozart then repeats the motif three times to form a longer melody, but each time the interval between the second and third notes of the motif gets larger. To complete the phrase, Mozart chooses a descending scalic pattern to complement the upwards-moving nature of the thrice played motif.

Here, Mozart is expanding one of the intervals within the motif each time it is played. The same technique could be applied by contracting one of the intervals in a similar manner.

The techniques used by the composer in this example are **intervallic expansion** and **extension**.

Breaking it up

Sometimes, composers build phrases or larger sections, not by building up melodies from motifs, but by taking a longer motif and then playing around with smaller fragments of that motif. For example, at the start of the first movement of his sixth symphony, Beethoven presents the following four bar idea:

In the bars that follow this four bar statement, the ideas are fragmented and then tossed around the strings of the orchestra; sometimes repeated, sometimes modified, sometimes repeated sequentially. Follow this score for the opening few bars of the symphony as you listen to CD 1, track 13.

Performance tasks

◆ Play through these three melodies. Identify the motif upon which each melody is built and identify the method that the composer has used to extend the motif into a longer melody.

◆ Now take these three motifs and develop them each, as indicated, to form a short melody.

sequence

repetition

intervallic expansion and extension

◆ Now compose your own short melodies using one or more of the techniques illustrated.

REACH

Cathy Dennis and Andrew Todd

On pages 23–4, we explored ways in which composers can create a melody by developing a small, single musical motif. The song *Reach*, which was a hit single for S Club 7 in 2000, is an excellent practical example of how composers can use all of these techniques to create a catchy, varied and extremely popular melody, whilst only using a small amount of musical material.

One of the co-composers of *Reach* is Cathy Dennis. In the late 1980s and early 1990s, Cathy had considerable chart success as a member of the disco band D-Mob and as a solo singer. Since her last chart success in 1997, she has been concentrating on composition and arrangements and has co-written a number of hit songs for S Club 7.

The verse of the song is based on two short ideas, which can be called **idea x** and **idea y**.

As you listen to the verse and follow the score, you will see how the composers have created the melody by repeating these two motifs, extending them, developing them sequentially and modifying them to fit with the lyrics.

Just before the chorus, the composers have written an ascending scalic passage that helps to build excitement and anticipation. Then, to mark the start of the chorus, we are introduced to a new musical idea, which, again, is two bars long.

This phrase is an antecedent phrase (see page 19) and is followed by a consequent phrase:

The chorus is created by repetition of these two ideas and by the extension of the consequent phrase. The chorus is rounded off with a concluding cadential phrase that leads into the instrumental introduction for verse two.

Listen to the recording of this song, which is on CD 1, track 14. Follow the following vocal score as you listen and take note of the text written above the staves. Also note that there is a ten bar instrumental introduction (not shown) and the singing starts at bar 11.

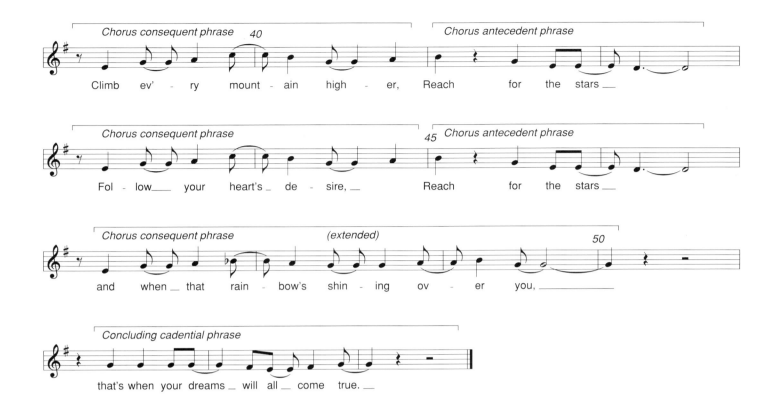

Chorus consequent phrase   40   Chorus antecedent phrase

Climb ev' - ry mount - ain high - er, Reach for the stars ___

Chorus consequent phrase   45   Chorus antecedent phrase

Fol - low ___ your heart's _ de - sire, ___ Reach for the stars ___

Chorus consequent phrase   (extended)   50

and when _ that rain - bow's shin - ing ov - er you, ___

Concluding cadential phrase

that's when your dreams _ will all _ come true. ___

Listening tasks

◆ At the start of the verse, **idea x** is heard six times in succession. Describe three techniques that the composers have employed to prevent the music from becoming too repetitive.
◆ How have the composers used the accompanying instruments to give life and energy to the song?

◆ What is the tonic key of this song?
◆ What key does the music modulate to in bar 19?
◆ The words of this song are very optimistic. How is this optimism reflected in the music?

In 1873, when he was 40 years old, Johannes Brahms composed a short set of variations on a theme that had been first used by Haydn for one of his *Divertimenti* for wind instruments. Brahms composed two versions of his variations: one for piano duet and one for full orchestra (featured on CD 1, track 15).

Before the nine variations are played, Brahms presents Haydn's original theme. In the orchestral version, this theme is played (appropriately) by the woodwind and horns. The theme is constructed using a small two-bar motif:

This two-bar motif can be divided into a number of even smaller motifs, for example, the dotted quaver-semiquaver idea in bar 1 and the two-crotchet idea in bar 2.

As you listen to the whole theme on CD 1, track 15 and follow the score, track the way that Brahms makes extensive usage of the ideas in the two-bar motif. You might like to use a coloured highlighter to show the different ideas at work on the score (providing this is your own copy of the book). You will be amazed at Haydn and Brahm's ingenuity, the piece is almost saturated with the motifs in its different forms.

Analysis tasks

◆ Which wind instruments are featured on this score?
◆ What does **Kl (B)** mean at the start of the score?
◆ Which wind instrument can be heard playing, but is not featured on this score?
◆ Which string instruments are also playing, but are not featured on the score?

◆ How are these string instruments being played?
◆ The following performance instructions are written on the score. What do they mean?
  i.   **Andante**
  ii. *ten.*
  iii. *dim.*
  iv. *smorz.*
◆ What do these signs mean?

   1.   **2.**

The term **Renaissance** is generally applied to Western art music composed during the period from 1450 to about 1600.

Types of Renaissance music

- Renaissance music fell into two styles – sacred music and secular music.
- Sacred vocal music was often performed without instrumental accompaniment and was often polyphonic in texture.
- Sacred vocal compositions included the vocal forms of **madrigal** and **chanson**.
- Secular instrumental music was often based on dance forms and rhythms. This music was often homophonic in texture.
- Keyboard and lute music was popular, with the *theme and variations* being a common form of composition.

Renaissance composers

- Palestrina (c. 1512–94) was the greatest composer of Renaissance church music. Other composers of sacred music included the Englishmen Thomas Tallis (c. between 1505 and 1510–85) and William Byrd (c. 1542 or 1543–1623).
- Thomas Weelkes (c. 1575–1623) was one of the best-known composers of madrigals.
- John Dowland (1562–1626) wrote many works for solo lute, as well as lute songs (vocal pieces with lute accompaniment).

Other historical and artistic events

- In 1453, the Hundred Years' War ended. (It had started in 1337!)
- In 1495, Leonardo da Vinci painted *The Last Supper.*
- In 1503, Leonardo da Vinci painted his *Mona Lisa.*

- In 1509, Henry VIII became King of England.
- In 1519, Charles V became Holy Roman Emperor.
- In 1534, Henry VIII separated the church in England from the Catholic Church.
- In 1549, Edward VI authorized the *Book of Common Prayer.*
- In 1558, Elizabeth I became the Queen of England.
- In 1571, the Battle of Lepanto took place.

Renaissance instruments

- Many instruments common in medieval times continued in use during the Renaissance. The viol family provided string sounds in instrumental ensembles, whilst the shawm (a precursor of the oboe), the recorder and the crumhorn were all popular wind instruments. The sackbut, an early version of the trombone, was a commonly used brass instrument.
- The lute was a popular instrument for both solo work and for accompanying songs. The virginal and harpsichord were both used widely across Europe, but particularly by English composers.

Features of Renaissance musical style

- Much Renaissance church music is **polyphonic** in texture. The music consists of a number of individual lines that are equal in their melodic importance. The music is also characterized by being performed *a cappella.*
- In contrast, much instrumental ensemble dance music, played by **consorts** of instruments, is homophonic in texture.
- In the Renaissance, the major/minor key system was still evolving from the modal system that had been used in the medieval period. Although much music sounded either major or minor, there were sometimes modal inflections, such as flattened seventh notes or semitonal clashes that were caused by the conflicts of the old modal system.

LA MOURISQUE FROM DANSERYE
Susato (c.1500–c.1560)

A man of many parts

Tielman (or Tylman) Susato lived in Antwerp between about 1500 and 1560 – his exact dates of birth and death are unknown. He was a multi-faceted musician and was involved in performing, composing and publishing music. One of his many published compositions was a selection of dance pieces for a consort (ensemble) of instruments, called *The Danserye*. Unlike a string quartet or a wind sextet, where specific instruments are designated to each part, Susato gave instructions that each part could be played by all or any kind of instrument. In practice, the four parts of each dance would probably have been played by a group of instruments from the same family – four viols, four sackbuts and shawms, or four recorders, perhaps. In addition, a percussion instrument, such as the tabor or nakers, would have played a simple ostinato rhythm to keep the ensemble in time. A recording of this piece can be found on CD 1, track 16.

Performance task

- *La Mourisque* is the first dance from *The Danserye*. Try performing the dance in a group of five, with one member of the group keeping the rhythmic ostinato on a suitable percussion instrument. It would be very effective to have the four-pitched parts played on instruments of the same family. If this is not possible, try to find the most effective way of blending your timbres together and keeping the melody as the forefront of the sound.

Rhythmic ostinato

How might you vary this rhythm during the course of the piece? Where might you vary the rhythm?

Part 1

Part 2

Part 3

Part 4

JACK AND JOAN
Campion (1567–1620)

During the Renaissance period, the madrigal was a popular song form in England and Italy. Madrigals were often sung *a cappella*. The term *a cappella* is literally translated from the Italian as 'at church', but in music, the term is generally used to mean any sort of vocal music that is sung unaccompanied, without instrumental accompaniment.

Try singing through this madrigal by the English composer Thomas Campion. Typically, it tells the tale of two hard-working people, Jack and Joan, who, presumably, are lovers, and the fun times that they have relaxing after a hard and honest day's work, dancing and enjoying themselves on the village green. Life was so much simpler in Renaissance times!

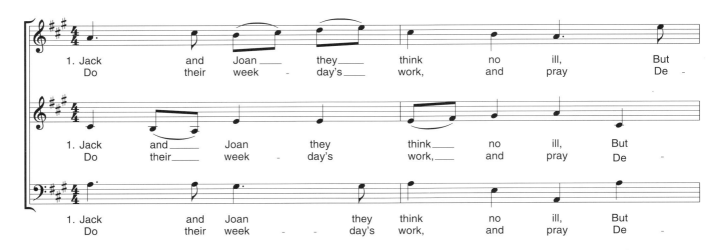

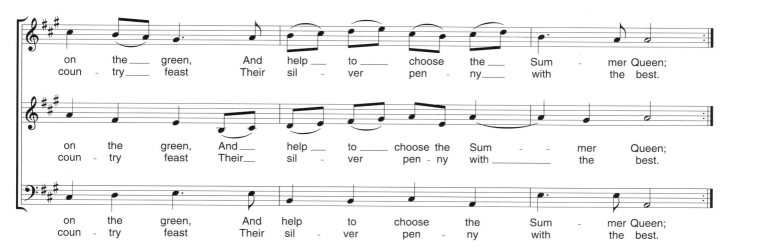

on   the ____ green,   And   help ____ to ____ choose   the ____ Sum - mer Queen;
coun - try ____ feast   Their   sil - ver   pen - ny ____ with   the   best.

on   the   green,   And ____   help ____ to ____   choose the   Sum - mer   Queen;
coun - try   feast   Their ____   sil - ver   pen - ny   with _____   the   best.

on   the   green,   And   help   to   choose   the   Sum - mer Queen;
coun - try   feast   Their   sil - ver   pen - ny   with   the   best.

THE BAROQUE STYLE
At-a-glance guide

The term **Baroque** is generally applied to Western art music composed during the period 1600–1750.

Types of Baroque music

◆ The first operas were heard during the Baroque period. Sacred (church) music compositions, such as the cantata and oratorio, were similar in musical style to operas, but took a religious text and theme and were not staged.

◆ Suites of dances for orchestra and for solo instruments were popular during the Baroque, and concertos were composed for groups of soloists and orchestra (**concerti grossi**) and for solo instruments and orchestra (**solo concerti**).

◆ Other types of composition for solo keyboard instruments included fugues and partitas. Compositions for a solo instrument and continuo accompaniment (**sonatas**) were popular, too.

Baroque composers

◆ Monteverdi (c. 1567–1643) started his career composing in the Renaissance style, but his main work secured the foundations of the Baroque style. Other Italian composers included Vivaldi (1678–1741), Corelli (1653–1713) and Torelli (1658–1709).

◆ German composers included Telemann (1681–1767), Handel (1685–1759), who worked in England for much of his career, and J.S. Bach (1685–1750).

◆ French composers included François Couperin (1668–1733) and Lully (1632–87).

◆ The greatest English composer was Henry Purcell (1658 or 1659–95).

Other historical and artistic events

◆ In 1588, the English defeated the Spanish Armada.

◆ In 1594, William Shakespeare wrote *Romeo and Juliet*.

◆ In 1624, Franz Hals painted *The Laughing Cavalier*.

◆ In 1666, the Great Fire of London followed the Great Plague of the previous year.

◆ In 1709, the first piano was built.

Baroque instruments

◆ The instrument most associated with the Baroque style is the harpsichord. This was a popular solo instrument and also the foundation of the Baroque orchestral sound, playing the continuo line, providing both harmony and rhythmic drive to the music.

◆ The organ remained popular for solo keyboard compositions and was also used as a continuo instrument.

◆ String instruments were developed from the viol family to the modern-day string family of instruments.

◆ Woodwind instruments developed, notably the flute and the recorder, which were still known as the **transverse flute** and the **flute á bec**. The oboe was a popular instrument together with its bass relation, the bassoon.

Features of Baroque musical style

◆ Dynamics are restricted to what is known as **stepped** or **terraced** shadings – that is, music should not change dynamic gradually (through a crescendo, for example), but rather step from one dynamic (*piano*) to another (*forte*).

◆ Melodies are built from short, usually one-bar motifs, rather than being in a longer phrase of, for example, four bars.

◆ It is characterized by a driving sense of rhythm. A rhythmic impetus that is always pushing the music forward.

◆ It can be highly ornamented with decorations. The trill, the turn and the mordent were particularly popular.

◆ It was in the Baroque period that tonality – the major/minor key system – became firmly established. From the major/minor key system, formal musical structures, such as binary form and rondo form, developed.

BRANDENBURG CONCERTO NO. 2 IN F MAJOR, 1ST MOVEMENT

Bach

Bach's Brandenburg Concertos

In project one, 'Forms and structures', we explored a dance movement in binary form by J.S. Bach. In addition to his four suites of dances for orchestra, Bach also composed six *Brandenburg Concertos* for orchestra. The concertos were dedicated by Bach to Duke Christian Ludwig of Brandenburg who, by all accounts, was himself a fine musician and employed a large orchestra at his court.

The *Brandenburg Concertos* are not solo concertos (for solo instrument and orchestra). They are all examples of the concerto grosso, where a small group of solo instruments are pitched against a larger orchestral group. In this concerto, the solo group consists of a violin, an oboe, a recorder and a piccolo trumpet, whilst the larger orchestral group (known as the **tutti** or the **ripieno**) is formed by the orchestral string section. Being a piece in the Baroque style, both the solo and the tutti group are accompanied by a cello and harpsichord continuo line.

Ritornello form

The movement featured here, the first movement of the second *Brandenburg Concerto*, is in **ritornello form**, a form much favoured by Baroque composers. Ritornello means, quite literally, 'little return'. The movement starts with a short eight bar theme that keeps returning throughout the movement:

In between the appearances of the theme, we hear short **interludes** that are usually played by one or more of the soloists. The first interlude that we hear after the first playing of the first theme is:

Form and tonality

Like Bach's *Gavotte* (in binary form) that we listened to earlier, ritornello form can also be defined by key. Although the first appearances of the ritornello and episode themes are in the tonic key of F major (as shown in the musical examples above), when they appear later in the movement, they are in different keys.

Using the plan on page 5 and the 'circle of fifths' wheel on page 6, draw up a key grid for this movement to show which keys Bach might modulate to.

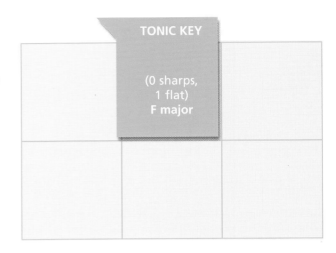

TONIC KEY

(0 sharps, 1 flat)
F major

Listening tasks

Now listen to the opening of this movement on CD 1, track 17.

Follow this chart, which tracks the order in which the ritornello theme and the interlude theme appears.

Bars	Theme	Key	Listening tasks
1–8	Ritornello	F major	How are the first two bars of the ritornello theme played? How does this change from bar 3 onwards?
9–10	Interlude	F major	Which solo instrument is featured in this interlude?
11–12	Ritornello	F major	Which two bars of the original ritornello theme are heard here?
13–14	Interlude	F major	Which solo instrument is featured in this interlude?
15–16	Ritornello		What key has the music modulated to?
17–18	Interlude		Which solo instrument is featured in this interlude?
19–20			Which idea is heard here?
21–2	Interlude		Which solo instrument is featured in this interlude? How else is this interlude different to the previous three interludes?

Other points to listen for

◆ Listen carefully to the cello/harpsichord continuo and in particular, the way that it supports the musical texture in both the solo and tutti sections.

◆ Listen to how the rhythmic drive of the music is never broken – it has perpetual motion.

◆ Listen for the distinctive sound of the piccolo trumpet and the way that it shines through the orchestral texture.

◆ Listen for the distinctive sound of the recorder and the way that it contrasts with the timbre of the other solo wind instrument, the oboe.

SOUND THE TRUMPET: COME, YE SONS OF ART, AWAY
Purcell (c.1658–95)

Henry Purcell was the greatest English composer of the Baroque era. He was employed at Westminster Abbey and the Chapel Royal, where he wrote church music. He also wrote an opera, *Dido and Aeneas*, and a number of special 'odes' for royal birthdays, marriages and funerals.

Sound the Trumpet is a movement from an ode composed for the birthday of Queen Mary in 1694. This movement is a duet in D major for two alto voices. Although it could be sung by women, it is likely that in Purcell's day it would have been sung by male altos, as it is on the recording that can be found on CD 1, track 18.

Accompanying the voices is a continuo line played by cello and harpsichord. The cello plays a **ground bass** line – a short (in this case, two bar) idea that is repeated over and over again throughout the piece.

As you listen to the piece, you will notice that, even when the music modulates to another key, the ground bass still plays.

Over this repeating bass line, the singers sing the words:

> *Sound the trumpet, sound the trumpet 'til around*
> *You make the list'ning shores abound.*
> *On the sprightly hautboy play!*
> *All the instruments of joy that skilful numbers can employ*
> *To celebrate the glories of this day.*

The singers sing antiphonally in a type of question and answer pattern, as shown below.

Listen to the whole piece, following the full score that can be found in the teacher's resource file.

Analysis tasks

- What is an 'hautboy'?
- What gives this piece a feeling of joy and celebration?
- How does Purcell paint the imagery of the words through the music that he has composed?
- With the bass line repeated again and again, this music could be very boring indeed. What has Purcell done to keep the listener's interest throughout the piece?

THE CLASSICAL STYLE
At-a-glance guide

Western art music styles

The term **Classical** is generally applied to Western art music composed during the period from 1750 to about 1820.

Types of Classical music

- Orchestral music took on a new importance in the Classical period, particularly through the development of the **symphony**.
- The solo concerto became most popular, with the piano concerto being the greatest in popularity.
- The string quartet became established as a chamber music ensemble.
- Opera continued to develop.
- Sacred (church) music became much grander, often accompanied by a full-scale orchestra.

Classical composers

- C.P.E. Bach (1714–88) and J.C. Bach (1735–82), sons of the great Baroque composer J.S. Bach, worked in a pre-Classical musical style known as the **empfindsamer stil** (the expressive style).
- The greatest composers of Classical music were Franz Josef Haydn (1732–1809) and Wolfgang Amadeus Mozart (1756–91).
- The compositional style of Beethoven (1770–1827) was founded in the Classical style, although in his later work, he laid the foundations of the Romantic musical style.

Other historical and artistic events
- In 1754, Dr Johnson published his *Dictionary*.
- In 1769, Watt patented his steam engine.
- In 1774, Louis XVI was crowned King of France. He lasted until 1792, when France was declared a republic.
- In 1776, the American Declaration of Independence took place.
- In 1788, John Fitch invented the steamboat.
- In 1798, Coleridge and Wordsworth published their *Lyrical Ballads*.

- In 1804, Napoleon was crowned Emperor of France.
- In 1805, the Battle of Trafalgar took place.
- In 1813, Jane Austen wrote *Pride and Prejudice*.
- In 1815, the Battle of Waterloo took place.

Classical instruments

- Although it was first produced during the Baroque period, composers first exploited the piano during the Classical period. The Classical piano had a wooden frame and therefore possessed less power and volume than modern instruments.
- Because of the rise of the piano, the harpsichord fell out of favour during the Classical period.
- The clarinet was introduced as a solo and orchestral instrument.
- Brass instruments continued to be valveless, but a greater range of notes was made possible in orchestral brass instruments through the use of varying sizes of crooks, which altered the fundamental pitch of an instrument.

Features of Classical music style

- Partly because of the introduction of the piano (and the piano's ability to shade dynamics through crescendi and diminuendi), dynamic contrast and graduations were a feature of Classical music.
- Melodic phrases became both longer and balanced. Typically, composers would write a four-bar question phrase, balanced by a four-bar answer phrase. The phrases are more properly know as the antecedent and consequent phrases.
- The major/minor system of tonality continued to be the foundation of musical forms and structures. Sonata form was built out of the relationship between the main key of the music (the **tonic**) and other closely related keys (such as the **dominant** and **subdominant**).
- Sonata form, which, like Classical melodies, was always balanced, was used as the foundation for symphonies, concertos and even operas.

46   *Heinemann GCSE Music, Student Book*

PIANO CONCERTO NO. 24 IN C MINOR, K491, 3RD MOVEMENT

Mozart

Mozart composed over twenty concertos for solo piano and orchestra. This concerto, which was composed in 1786, was one of only two concertos by Mozart that were in minor keys.

Mozart's mature concertos were composed to a three-movement plan. As with a symphony, the first movements were written in sonata form and the second movements were generally slow movements. The form of the last movements usually favoured sonata form, rondo form and sonata-rondo form. However, Mozart sometimes built his concerto final movements as a **Theme and variations**, as he did in this piano concerto.

Listen to the extracts that are provided on CD 1, track 19, and follow through this analysis of the theme and five of the variations as you listen.

Theme

The movement starts, as one would expect, with the theme, which is played in the string section of the orchestra, with doublings in the woodwind, but without the piano. It is on CD 1, track 19, starting at 0.00.

Listening tasks

◆ What is the tonic key of this theme?
◆ Which key has the theme modulated to at the middle double bar?
◆ What is the form of the theme?
◆ Look through the score of the theme and identify a descending chromatic line.
◆ How has Mozart built his melodies out of motifs?

Performance task

◆ Make and perform a four-part arrangement, or make and perform a piano reduction of Mozart's theme.

Variation 1

The first variation on CD 1, track 19 (starting at 0.51), features the solo piano accompanied by the strings. The piano part starts:

◆ How do the strings accompany this solo piano line?
◆ Which elements of the theme are maintained or developed in *Variation 1*?

Variation 2

This variation, on CD 1, track 19 (starting at 1.40), starts with just the woodwind section (flute, oboes, clarinets and bassoons):

- ◆ Which elements of the theme are maintained or developed in *Variation 2*?
- ◆ What happens when the first half of the variation is repeated?

Variation 3

This variation, on CD 1, track 19 (starting at 2.29), starts with just the solo piano playing:

- ◆ What are the new rhythmic ideas that are added in this variation?
- ◆ What happens when the first half of the variation is repeated?

Variation 4

Listen to this variation, on CD 1, track 19 (starting at 3.20), without the benefit of a score.

- ◆ How is this variation totally different from the theme and three variations that precede it?

Variation 5

Listen to this variation, on CD 1, track 19 (starting at 4.14), without the benefit of a score.

- ◆ How is this variation totally different from the theme and four variations that precede it?

SYMPHONY NO. 103, 4TH MOVEMENT

Haydn (1732–1809)

Alongside his 24 piano concertos, Mozart composed 41 symphonies. But it was Franz Joseph Haydn who was classed as the 'father' of the Classical symphony, writing 104 of them in total. Through these symphonies, the standard four-movement form, the Classical symphonic form and the Classical symphony orchestra were developed and established.

By the end of the Classical period, symphonies were being composed in a standard four-movement pattern. The first movement, at a moderate-fast speed (occasionally with a slow introduction), was in sonata form. There then followed a slower movement, then a dance movement in 3/4 time (usually a minuet or trio), and finally another fast movement, which could be in sonata form, rondo form or sonata-rondo form.

Listen to CD 1, track 20, which features the start of the last movement from Haydn's 103rd symphony. The symphony is scored for the standard Classical orchestra of two each of flutes, oboes, clarinets and bassoons, French horns and trumpets. Two timpani provide the sole percussion and the full string section completes the orchestral line up.

The score shown here is a piano reduction of the orchestral score for the first 27 bars of this movement. As you listen, notice the way that, in the Classical style, every aspect of the music is balanced. Notice the balanced phrasing (four-bar antecedent phrases, four-bar consequent phrases), the balance between the wind/brass and the strings, and the balance between upper and lower strings. Finally, notice the clever manner in which Haydn manipulates the musical material, alternating it between the instruments of the orchestra.

THE ROMANTIC STYLE
At-a-glance guide

The term **Romantic** is generally applied to Western art music composed during the period from 1820 to about 1900, although many composers produced Romantic-style music well into the twentieth century.

Types of Romantic music

◆ The symphony continued to develop and expand, as did the orchestra. In particular, the woodwind, brass and percussion sections grew to include a greater range of timbres and pitches.

◆ As well as 'absolute' music, composers also began to favour 'programme' music – music that told a story or depicted a descriptive scene or event.

◆ In contrast, smaller more intimate forms of music became popular, such as the **lied** (song) and the piano miniature.

◆ Opera continued to develop, albeit on a much greater scale.

◆ The solo concerto continued in popularity, with the piano concerto still a particular favourite with composers.

Romantic composers

◆ After Beethoven the great Austro-German composers were Mendelssohn (1809–47), Schubert (1797–1828), Schumann (1810–56) and Brahms (1833–97).

◆ Tchaikovsky (1840–93) was the greatest Russian Romantic composer.

◆ Berlioz (1803–69) was the greatest French Romantic composer.

◆ In Italy, Rossini (1792–1868) is best known for his operas.

Other historical and artistic events

◆ In 1830, the first railway was built from Liverpool to Manchester.

◆ In 1838, Charles Dickens wrote *The Pickwick Papers*.

◆ In 1841, Adolph Sax invented the saxophone.

◆ In 1858, London's Covent Garden Opera House was opened.

◆ In 1864, Lewis Carroll wrote *Alice's Adventures in Wonderland*.

◆ In 1876, Alexander Graham Bell invented the telephone.

◆ In 1877, Edison invented the phonograph, the precursor of all modern recording equipment.

◆ In 1888, Van Gogh painted his *Sunflowers*.

◆ In1901, Queen Victoria died. She had been queen since 1837.

Romantic instruments

◆ The Industrial Revolution had a considerable impact on music. Iron (as opposed to wooden) frames became the norm for pianos, which meant that the instruments became more robust and able to play louder music, thus giving composers a wider range of expressive possibilities.

◆ Woodwind instruments began to adopt keyed systems, which meant that players had a wider range of notes and were able to play with greater dexterity and fluency.

◆ Similarly, brass instruments were built with valve systems, which meant that players were able to play with the full range of chromatic notes.

◆ The percussion section of the orchestra expanded, too, to include both pitched and unpitched instruments.

Features of Romantic musical style

◆ Romantic melodies are often long, expansive lines with lyrical and expressive qualities.

◆ Orchestral textures are generally much thicker than Classical orchestral textures. The greater range of orchestral colours and timbres available meant that composers could paint more colourful sound pictures.

◆ Dynamics and expressive markings in orchestral and chamber music scores were more detailed in the Romantic period.

◆ Harmonies and melodies became more chromatic during the Romantic period, with the consequence that the major/minor key system, which had become so important to musical structure during the Baroque and Classical periods, began to lose some of its stability.

PRELUDE IN C MINOR
Chopin (1810–49)

ℹ **Composer in exile**

From an early age, it was clear that Frédéric Chopin possessed an extraordinary talent as both a pianist and composer. When he was twenty, it became clear that if he wanted to realize his true musical potential, he would have to live and work abroad (rather than in Poland, where he was born). He worked in various European cities including Vienna, Stuttgart and London, but his main home away from Poland was Paris.

Chopin composed some orchestral music, but his main compositional output was for his own instrument, the piano. He composed over 150 pieces for solo piano. Apart from lengthier works, such as his three piano sonatas, he composed many miniatures, shorter compositions that economically encapsulated a particular mood or emotion (in true Romantic fashion), as well as exploiting the ever-increasing potential of the piano. When you come to play Chopin's piano music, you will have no doubt that he knew exactly how to write for the instrument from his own practical experience.

Follow through this score as you listen to Chopin's *Prelude in C minor*, on CD 1, track 21.

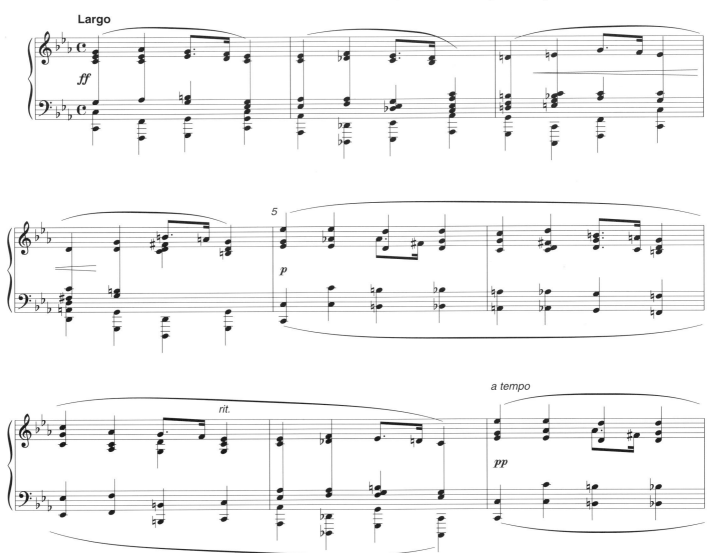

Analysis tasks

- What is the general texture of this piece?
- What key is this piece in?
- What key does the music modulate to at the end of bars 2, 3 and 4? (It may help to draw up a key grid for the piece to use as you answer this question.)
- What is the main feature of the bass line in bars 5–6?
- What is the overall form of this piece?
- What do you notice about the way that Chopin has organized the dynamics in this piece?

- What do you notice about the way that Chopin has organized the tempo in this piece?
- From the pianist's point of view, what do you notice about the way that this piece has been written? (Look carefully at the music to be played by both the left and right hands.)
- This piece is only thirteen bars long, but it is packed with musical detail and concentrates a great deal of expressiveness and emotion within the music. What mood or emotion do you think Chopin was trying to express in this piece? Give musical reasons for your opinion.

As we know, the term 'Romantic music' means much more than an association with romantic love. Composers expressing a wide range of human emotions and expressiveness through their work characterize music of the Romantic period.

Nevertheless, this piece by Peter Ilyich Tchaikovsky, which is based on Shakespeare's play *Romeo and Juliet*, does provide an expansive musical expression of human love, as well as being an excellent example of the Romantic musical style.

There are a number of contrasting musical themes in this work that represent the different dramatic strands of the play. There is a solemn, homophonic hymn-like idea, which is heard at the start and the end of the piece to represent Friar Lawrence. There is a strident, fast and aggressive theme to represent the battles between the Montague and Capulet families that run throughout the course of the play.

The theme that represents the forbidden love between Romeo and Juliet also appears several times in the piece. It is first heard as a duet on the mellow sounding cor anglais and violas. It is then heard on the flutes and oboes. Follow this woodwind score as you listen to the recording on CD 1, track 22.

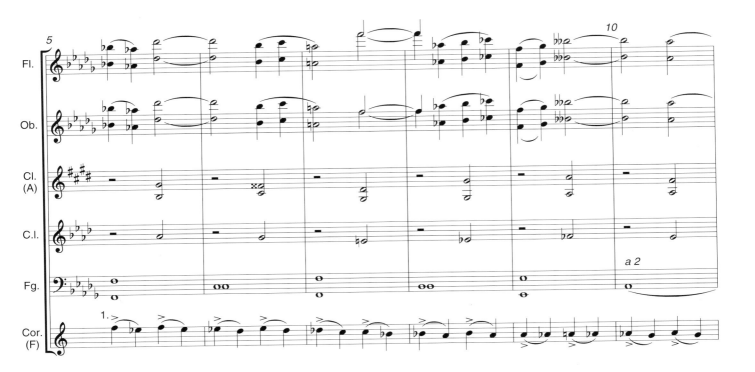

Analysis tasks

- Tchaikovsky has written the following performance instructions on the score:
  - *dolce ma sensibile*
  - *espress.*
- What do these terms mean? Why has Tchaikovsky written them on the score?
- What textural features do you notice about the flute and oboe melody line?
- Look at and listen carefully to the horn part. Describe the music played by the horns and describe the effect that this music has in the overall musical texture.

- How does the music played by the clarinets, cor anglais and bassoons contrast with the flute, oboe and horn lines?
- Whilst this music is being played in the woodwind, what is happening in the string section of the orchestra?
- Which features of this music identify it as depicting the emotion of love? Give musical reasons for your answer.
- Now listen to Chopin's *Prelude in C minor* and the love theme from *Romeo and Juliet*. Which features of these two pieces identify them as being from the Romantic era? As always, give musical reasons for your answer.

Carnival music

Although he was born and bred in New York, the jazz saxophonist Sonny Rollins was brought up by parents who hailed from the US Virgin Islands where there is a famous tradition of carnival at the end of April every year.

The Virgin Islands Carnival website (www.stthomas.com/carnival) paints a vivid picture of St Thomas at carnival time:

> Give yourself the gift of Carnival in the Spring and get into the spirit of revelry on the island of St Thomas in the United States Virgin Islands, the American Paradise. It is a dazzling cultural tour that can last one week, two weeks or one month. Enjoy unique traditions and some exotic foods Caribbean style. Come and immerse yourself in some enchanting and truly unforgettable events such as J'ouvert (dancing in the streets of Charlotte Amalie) from midnight until dawn.
>
> Come to the Virgin Islands Carnival this Spring, on the island of St Thomas, where the celebration transcends 'Festival'. During the last two weeks of April, the hills of St Thomas reverberate with the calypso rhythms of brass, steel, and scratch bands, as locals and visitors celebrate the annual US Virgin Islands Carnival.

Don't stop the carnival

In the 1952 St Thomas carnival, road marches were introduced for the first time. Unfortunately, this innovation coincided with a particularly rainy season and many of the marching musicians got soaked. Many of the revellers were in colourful paper costumes that were ruined by the heavy downpour. However, because of the singing, the high spirits of the masqueraders were not dampened by the rains.

One of the musicians, a Trinidadian calypso king named 'The Duke of Iron', started to improvise a song he had made up on the spot called *Rain, Don't Stop the Carnival*. His singing was contagious and soon everyone in the parade took up the song and sang it throughout the mile-long procession.

Possibly inspired by the marchers and The Duke of Iron's famous song, Sonny Rollins himself composed a song called *Don't Stop the Carnival*. There is a recording of Sonny Rollins leading a performance of this song on CD 1, track 23. Listen to the recording and follow some of the ideas that are represented on this score of the first three bars of the piece.

Listening to the recording, you will hear some of the traditional calypso rhythms typical of the music heard at the Virgin Islands carnivals. On the *Heinemann GCSE Music CD-ROM*, there is a sequenced version of *Don't Stop the Carnival* that includes typical Caribbean rhythms that would be played on the congos and agogo bells. When notated, a typical rhythm might be:

St Thomas

Another of Sonny Rollins' well-known compositions is *St Thomas*, named after the capital of the US Virgin Islands where the carnival is held.

The piece is based around a simple but syncopated sixteen-bar melody (including whole bars of rests), harmonized in an interesting way using seventh chords and other added harmonies. Listen to Sonny Rollins playing *St Thomas* on CD 1, track 24.

As you can see from the score, this tune is in the key of C major, but the chords used to harmonize the tune are not as straightforward. Every single chord is an 'added' chord – the usual diatonic triad has at least one extra note added to it. Here is a breakdown of each chord. You might find it useful to play each chord on a keyboard or guitar as you go through the table.

Chord	Basic triad	Added notes/altered notes
C6	C major (C, E, G)	A – the sixth note above C
Em7	E minor (E, G, B)	D – the seventh note above D
A7	A major (A, C sharp, E)	G – the seventh note above A
Dm7	D minor (D, F, A)	C – the seventh note above D
G7	G major (G, B, D)	F – the seventh note above G
Em7 (flat 5)	E minor (E, G, B)	D – the seventh note above D **and** the B becomes B flat
B flat 7	B flat (B flat, D, F)	A flat – the seventh note above B flat
A flat 7 (sharp 5)	A flat (A flat, C, E flat)	G – the seventh note above A flat **and** the E flat becomes E natural
C7	C major (C, E, G)	B flat – the seventh note above C
C9/E	C major (C, E, G)	D – the ninth note above C **and** B the seventh note above C flat; **and** the bass note is an E
F6	F major (F, A, C)	D – the sixth note above F
F#o7	This is the diminished chord of F sharp – F sharp, A, C, E flat	
C6/G	C major (C, E, G)	A – the sixth note above C and the bass note is a G

Performance tasks

St Thomas is an excellent tune to use as the basis for a group performance with improvisation. Try organizing your performance using this plan:

◆ Divide into two groups – those of you who will play the tune and/or will improvise on the tune, and those of you who will provide the 'rhythm' section (keyboards, guitars, bass, drums and percussion).

◆ Members of the rhythm section could work out a 'foundation' rhythm pattern based on the patterns shown on page 57. Get this rhythm going and then add the chords (keyboards and guitars) and a bass line that ties in with the rhythmic patterns played by the drums and percussion.

◆ Melody instruments should start by playing the tune through in unison. The melodic rhythm given to you on page 57 should only be a guide. When you get a feel for the music, your melodic rhythm will be looser than the notation suggests. However, make sure that you keep the overall rhythmic co-ordination of the melody instruments as tight as possible.

◆ When you can play the melody in unison, try putting in some harmonies. You might find that the short, staccato nature of the first two lines lends itself well to unison playing, whilst the third line and the first two bars of the last line would work well with some melodic harmony. Perhaps the last bar of the melody would sound more powerful and punchy if played in unison. Try a variety of solutions.

◆ When you have worked through these initial stages, put everything together, playing through the sixteen-bar tune twice.

◆ Assuming that everything is working really well, try some improvisation. Keeping the chord sequence unchanged, try improvising your own melodies over the top. Some ways of improvising might be:
  • Keeping the melodic rhythm the same as on the score, but using a contrasting pitch shape.
  • Keeping the melodic pitch shape the same as on the score, but using a different rhythmic pattern.
  • Playing the same melody as on the score, but adding melodic 'fill-ins' at the end of each phrase during the rest bars.
  • Your drummer and/or percussionist might like to take a verse for improvisation too, with everyone else playing a short 'stab' chord at the beginning of each phrase.

◆ Take lots of time to experiment with different improvisations and encourage everyone to have a go.

◆ For your final performance of *St Thomas*, agree on a format. You could start with a four-bar percussive introduction and have everyone playing the tune through twice, then have a series of improvisatory verses. To end the piece, you could have everyone playing through the tune for a final time. The secret is to work out your own plan.

◆ You might like to give your performance a really authentic feel by performing it 'on the move', as it would be in a carnival procession. Obviously, you will have to come to some sort of arrangement for your pianist or keyboard player, but be imaginative. How about performing *St Thomas* in assembly, entering from the back of the hall and processing through the assembled ranks? (Check with your Headteacher or Head of Year first!)

Like carnival, *St Thomas* is to be enjoyed, so enjoy it!

LE CARNAVAL ROMAIN
Berlioz (1803–69)

Roman carnivals

In medieval and Renaissance Rome, there was a strong tradition of carnival. Originally, the Roman carnivals had been linked to pagan rites, such as the coming of spring and the celebration of fertility. Later, the celebrations extended to paying tribute to Roman gods, such as Bacchus (the god of wine) and Lupercus (the god of fertility). As you might imagine, these carnivals were, by the very nature of the themes that they were celebrating, extremely lively affairs with a good deal of debauchery and mischief.

As the Catholic Church established a greater influence over all aspects of life, the spring carnival became more and more associated with the start of the Lenten season, and, in particular, with Shrove Tuesday. It is from this that the tradition of the 'Mardi Gras' comes, a tradition that can be found in many parts of the world and especially those where Catholicism is or has been an important influence.

Berlioz's Roman carnival

In 1838, Hector Berlioz's opera *Benvenuto Cellini* was first produced in Paris. The opera is about a young sculptor (Benvenuto Cellini) who has been commissioned by the Pope to cast a new statue. There are a number of subplots within the opera involving love, treachery and deceit, and the whole opera takes place against the backdrop of Rome on Shrove Tuesday and Ash Wednesday (the start of the Lenten period).

Five years after the opera was first produced, Berlioz took some melodies from the opera and made them into a concert overture that he called *Le Carnaval Romain* (Roman Carnival). In the overture, Berlioz captures in music the excitement, dancing and mayhem that characterized the great Roman spring celebration.

Listen to the two extracts from the opera that are on CD 1, track 25 and track 26.

The first extract features a solo for the cor anglais that comes near the start of the overture:

The second extract features a melody that is played by the woodwind and the first violins in unison:

Listening tasks

◆ What are the musical differences between the two extracts?
◆ What aspects of *Le Carnaval Romain* do you think each of the two extracts/melodies represent?
◆ Which elements of the music are important in helping Berlioz to re-create the atmosphere of *Le Carnaval Romain*?

There is a further set of tasks for you to complete on *Le Carnaval Romain* in the teacher's resource file.

ZADOK THE PRIEST
Handel (1685–1759)

Coronation music

George Frideric Handel composed the anthem *Zadok the Priest* for the coronation of King George II and Queen Caroline in Westminster Abbey on 11 October 1727. The words are taken from the First Book of Kings in The Old Testament:

> *Zadok the Priest and Nathan the Prophet*
> *   anointed Solomon King.*
> *And all the people rejoiced and said:*
> *'God save the King! Long live the King!*
> *May the King live forever.*
> *Alleluia! Amen!'*

The anthem is in three sections. Listen to the recording of *Zadok the Priest* on CD 1, track 27. Follow the music below as you listen and answer the questions that relate to each section of music.

Section 1

The anthem starts with a section for the orchestra alone.

◆ At the start of a special occasion, such as a coronation, there is bound to be a sense of excitement and anticipation. How does the composer create this sense of excitement and anticipation through the music at the start of *Zadok the Priest*? Pay particular attention to the way that Handel uses dynamics, rhythm, the bass notes and the arpeggio figures to create the atmosphere.

When the singers first enter, they proclaim:

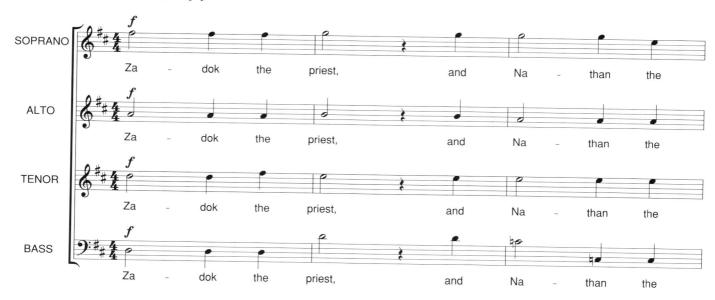

◆ The texture of the music sung by the choir is homophonic – all four parts are singing to exactly the same rhythm in 'block' chords. What is the orchestra playing underneath this vocal music?

◆ The first entry by the choir is very dramatic. How does Handel create the sense of drama, grandeur and power through his music?

Section 2

This section features the words 'And all the people rejoiced'.

◆ What is the metre (time signature) of this section?
◆ Which word is treated melismatically (with several notes to a syllable) in this section?
◆ Where can you hear a dotted rhythm in this section?

Section 3

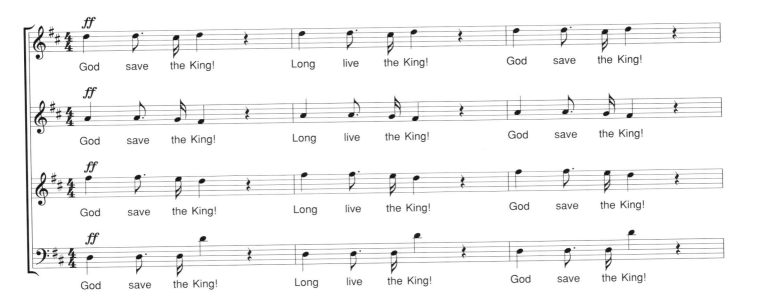

◆ What is the orchestra playing underneath this vocal music?
◆ How does Handel's music create the atmosphere and feeling of a large crowd of people proclaiming the anointing of a new king?
◆ How do the rhythms of this section contrast with the rhythms of the opening section ('Zadok the priest ...')?

After this proclamation, the choir sings the words 'Alleluia! Amen!'

◆ These words are repeated many times. Describe some of the different ways that Handel sets these words to music.
◆ What is the final cadence of the anthem (on the word 'Alleluia!')? Chose from perfect, imperfect, plagal and interrupted.

CROWN IMPERIAL
William Walton (1902–83)

William Walton composed his march *Crown Imperial* for the coronation of King George VI and Queen Elizabeth in Westminster Abbey on 12 May 1937.

Listen to the recording of *Crown Imperial* on CD 1, track 28. Follow the table below as you listen and answer the questions that relate to each section of the music.

Section 1

◆ At the start of a special occasion, such as a coronation, there is bound to be a sense of excitement and anticipation. How does the composer create this sense of excitement and anticipation through the music at the start of *Crown Imperial*?

Pay particular attention to the way that he uses dynamics, rhythm (particularly syncopation), the bass notes and orchestration (the use of the different instruments in the orchestra) to create the atmosphere.

Section 2

◆ When the theme that started section 1 comes back, the excitement and anticipation has increased. How does the composer 'wind up' the atmosphere in a musical manner?

Once again, pay particular attention to the way that he uses dynamics, rhythm (particularly syncopation), the bass notes and orchestration (the use of the different instruments in the orchestra) to create the atmosphere.

Section 3

◆ Which family of instruments plays this new idea? At what dynamic do they play? What effect does this new idea have on the atmosphere of the music?

Section 4

◆ When this idea is heard for the first time, the mood of the music changes. Which family of instruments plays this theme the first time that it is heard?
◆ What is the dynamic when this idea is heard for the first time?
◆ What happens to the tonality (key) of the music when this idea enters?
◆ What happens to the tempo of the music when this idea is introduced?
◆ What is the texture of the music at this point? Is it monophonic, homophonic or polyphonic?
◆ How does the rhythm of this idea contrast with the rhythm of the music in the opening section of *Crown Imperial*?
◆ What particular aspect of a coronation atmosphere do you think the composer is attempting to portray in this section of music?

Further work

◆ Imagine the coronation scene in Westminster Abbey – full of pomp, ceremony and tradition, and a thoroughly 'British' occasion. How effectively do you think William Walton managed to capture the atmosphere and spirit of the coronation through his music? In your answer, refer to as many different aspects of the music as you are able.

◆ *Zadok the Priest* and *Crown Imperial* were both composed especially for the coronations of British monarchs. Do the two pieces have any similar characteristics in the way that they create a sense of pomp, majesty and grandeur?

YOM HOLEDET (HAPPY BIRTHDAY)

Gabriel Butler, Ya'akov Lamaia, Jacky Oved and Moshe Datz

Music for birthday celebrations

Happy Birthday to You must be one of the most well-known pieces of music ever composed, as the song is known the whole world over. In fact, along with *Happy Birthday* by Stevie Wonder, it probably is *the* song that is sung at birthday parties and celebrations.

As an alternative, listen to this song with the title *Happy Birthday*. The song was composed in 1999 and has lyrics in English and Hebrew. It is performed by the band Eden on CD 1, track 29.

(Happy birthday, happy birthday)
Ze ha-yom la-khalom, niganev beyakhad
It's a celebration, ze ba li pa'am ba-shana

Happy birthday to you, khalomot yitgashmu
'Im nakhgog ve-nirkod 'ad ha-boker ('Od nakhlom)
Happy birthday to you, she-ha-shanim ya'avru
Be-kef, be-simkha u-ve-'osher always
(Come on, break it, drum it out)

Yeladim mizdaknim (Oh yeah …)
'Od shana' overet (Hey …)
It's a celebration, ze ba li pa'am ba-shana

Happy birthday to you, khalomot yitgashmu
'Im nakhgog ve-nirkod 'ad ha-boker ('Od nakhlom)
Happy birthday to you, she-ha-shanim ya'avru
Be-kef, be-simkha u-ve-'osher always

Listening tasks

- The song is performed by the group Eden. What sort of ensemble is Eden?
- The opening line ('Happy birthday, happy birthday') has the voices treated electronically, through a **vocoder**. What is the effect that this process has on the voices?
- Sometimes the individual singers sing as soloists, sometimes two or more singers sing in unison, and sometimes the singers sing in harmony. Whereabouts do these types of singing occur? (Refer to the lyrics printed above.)
- How is the lyric 'Come on, break it, drum it out' delivered by the singer?
- How has the instrumental backing for the singers been created? Which accompanying instruments are used?
- What is it about this song that would make it good to play at a large family party or celebration?

Think particularly about the melody, in particular, the chorus, and the ease with which it could be sung by a large group of people. Also think about the beat and how easy it would be for people to dance along to the music. Although this piece dates from 1999 and is clearly influenced by contemporary dance rhythms, do you think that it would appeal to people of different ages? Why/why not?

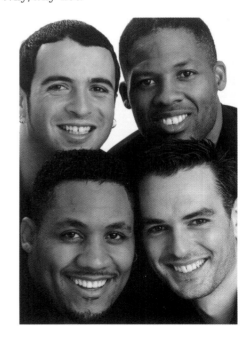

WEDDING MARCH FROM A MIDSUMMER NIGHT'S DREAM

Mendelssohn (1809–47)

Wedding music

In 1843, the King of Prussia commissioned Felix Mendelssohn to compose some incidental music for a performance of Shakespeare's play *A Midsummer Night's Dream* to be held at the King's palace at Potsdam. As a result of this commission, we now have what is probably the most played and requested piece of wedding music of all time.

Mendelssohn's *Wedding March* was originally intended to be played as incidental music between Acts IV and V of Shakespeare's play, depicting the marriages between Theseus and Hippolyta, Demetrius and Helena, and Lysander and Hermia.

Listen to the extract from Mendelssohn's *Wedding March* on CD 1, track 30.

The very first thing that we hear in the march tells us that something very important is about to happen. Three trumpets play a fanfare, an upwardly rising arpeggio played to an insistent triplet rhythm.

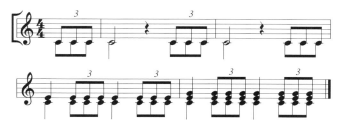

Immediately after this fanfare, the full orchestra enters – *fortissimo* – with a forceful, homophonic texture and a melody that is built from dotted rhythms, trills and yet more arpeggio figures.

Later in the march, we hear a softer, more lyrical theme that depicts the love and the romance of a wedding.

Analysis tasks

Using musical technical language, answer these two questions giving musical reasons for your views.

- Why is Mendelssohn's music so appropriate for a special, celebratory occasion such as a marriage?
- What makes the music so memorable that so many people have wanted it played at their own weddings?

Performance tasks

- Try your own performance of the opening section of Mendelssohn's *Wedding March*, using the five parts printed here. Note that the 'fanfare' part splits into three, so you will need at least three players on this part. You will also need to add your own dynamics and phrasing.

Fanfare

Part 1

Part 2

Part 3

Part 4

Funeral music

On page 45, we explored music composed by Henry Purcell for the birthday of Queen Mary in 1694. A year later, in 1695, Purcell found himself having to compose some quite different music for Queen Mary's funeral and, ironically, the same music was played at Purcell's own funeral just ten months later.

On CD 1, tracks 31 and 32, you can hear extracts from two of the instrumental pieces that Purcell composed for this most solemn of occasions. Both extracts are scored for a large brass ensemble and, as you would expect, both extracts are in minor keys. However, the textures of the two extracts are different.

The first piece, on CD 1, track 31, which is called *March*, has a homophonic texture where the brass instruments play together in a block chordal texture.

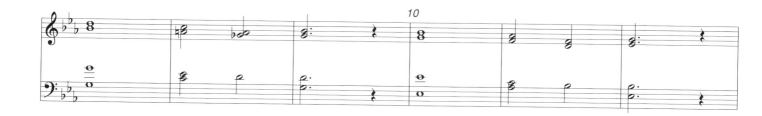

The second piece, on CD 1, track 32, is called *Canzona* and has a different texture, with each brass instrument having an individual line that plays against the other lines in the ensemble. Although all of the instruments play in crotchets, each individual line can be heard, as opposed to the 'block chord' sound of the march.

THREE LIONS

Ian Brodie, David Baddiel and Frank Skinner

In 1996, England played host to Euro '96, the first major international football tournament to be played in England since the World Cup victory of 1966. To mark the occasion, Ian Brodie, of the group The Lightning Seeds, teamed up with the entertainers David Baddiel and Frank Skinner to produce the song *Three Lions*.

Not only did the song reach number one in the charts, it was also adopted by fans on the terraces as the favourite chant sung at all of England's games in the tournament.

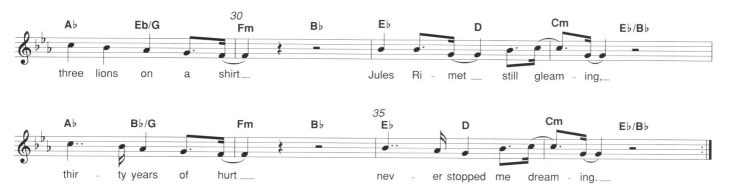

three lions on a shirt___ Jules Ri - met ___ still gleam - ing,___

thir - ty years of hurt ___ nev - er stopped me dream - ing.___

As you will quickly realize when you sing the song, the melody is made up of just a few simple motifs that are repeated over and over again. Also, the pitch range of the melody is quite narrow, the 'It's coming home' refrain only uses four pitches with a total range of a fifth. These could well be the reasons why fans on the terraces found the song so easy to sing.

Other football songs or chants have been adapted or copied from popular songs. Particular songs have been adopted by individual clubs, for example:

◆ *I'm Forever Blowing Bubbles* – West Ham United
◆ *You'll Never Walk Alone* – Liverpool
◆ *Blue Moon* – Manchester City.

TWO SALTERELLOS
From the fourteenth and nineteenth centuries

Listen to CD 2, track 1. The recording is of a fourteenth-century dance by an anonymous Italian composer. The dance is called a **salterello**, a name derived from the Italian word 'salto' meaning jump, which is most appropriate for a dance that is lively and involved the dancers leaping and jumping around.

As you listen follow this representation of the melody line:

The recording is of a performance given on original, authentic instruments of the fourteenth century. The melody is played on the shawm, a double-reeded instrument that preceded the oboe. Under the melody you can hear a drone played by a trumpet and rhythmic accompaniment is provided by a tambourine, a tabor and a pair of nakers.

Listening tasks

Which of the following patterns best represents the music played by the tambourine at the start of the salterello?

(✕ = Hit, ᴡ = Shake)

(a)

(b)

(c)

(d)

◆ How does the music played by the shawm differ later in the piece?
◆ How does the rhythmic accompaniment change later in the piece?
◆ What makes this music suitable for dancing to? Copy the following chart into your book and describe the musical characteristics that create the dance-like qualities in the music.

Rhythm and metre	
Melody	
Tempo	
Harmony/timbre/texture	

Now listen to CD 2, track 2. The recording is of the last movement of Mendelssohn's fourth symphony, which is sometimes known as the 'Italian' symphony.

Mendelssohn labelled this movement *Salterello*, *Presto*. Follow this score of the first few bars as you listen to the recording.

Listening tasks

◆ As you did with the fourteenth century salterello, think about what identifies Mendelssohn's music as being music for or about dancing. Again, copy this chart into your book and describe the musical characteristics that create the dance-like qualities in the music.

Rhythm and metre	
Melody	
Tempo	
Harmony/timbre/texture	

◆ Using the chart below, compare the two salterellos. Complete the boxes with appropriate statements.

◆ These two pieces were composed approximately 500 years apart. Which elements of each piece identify the date of composition and which elements of each piece could you regard as being 'universal', shared by both styles and eras of music?

	Medieval salterello	Mendelssohn's salterello
Metre	The music is in common (4/4) time.	
Tonality	The music is in a minor mode.	The music is in the key of …
Melody	The main melodic idea is played on a reeded woodwind instrument, the shawm.	
Harmony	The trumpet plays a drone that keeps a constant tonic note throughout the piece.	
Rhythm	The tambourine, tabor and nakers play constant, distinctive rhythmic ostinato patterns throughout the piece.	

Suites of dances

In project one, 'Forms and structures', we performed and analysed a gavotte by J.S. Bach. Bach, like many other composers, composed many suites of dances – collections of independent movements with dance characteristics. These dances included the gavotte, bourrée and passepied from France, the jig from Britain, the allemande from Germany, the sarabande from Spain and the polonaise from Poland.

Although these dances formed independent movements within the suite, they were usually bound together by key (every dance in a suite was composed in the same key) and they were usually all in binary form.

A practical composer

Bach composed suites for solo keyboard and for solo, unaccompanied cello as well as for orchestra. His four orchestral suites all contain parts for strings and continuo, as you would expect in Baroque orchestral music. In addition, each orchestral suite features a different combination of woodwind and brass instruments.

The first suite has parts for two oboes and a bassoon; the second features a solitary flute in addition to the strings and continuo; the third includes three trumpets, two oboes and timpani. The fourth expands to include three trumpets, three oboes, timpani and bassoon. Bach was an extremely practical composer and composed music suitable for the players that he had available at the time of composition – good advice for any budding composer.

This bourrée is from Bach's *Orchestral Suite No. 2 in B minor*. Before you listen to the recording of the piece, go back to project one and remind yourself about binary form. Remember that:

◆ binary form is a bi-partite (two-part) form that can be expressed A B.
◆ keys and modulations define the structure of binary form. Remember that in binary form, the music usually modulates away from the tonic key at the end of section A and back to the tonic key by the end of section B.

Now listen to the recording of Bach's bourrée on CD 2, track 3, following the score as you listen.

Performance tasks

- As you did with the gavotte, make your own arrangement and performance of this bourrée. All the parts are given to you at concert pitch. Remember to transpose if necessary.
- The CD-ROM that accompanies *Heinemann GCSE Music* has a sequenced version of this movement without the solo line so that you can play along as the soloist.
- Alternatively, there is a task on the CD-ROM that requires you to create a harpsichord continuo part for the movement.

Analysis tasks

- This bourrée is in the key of B minor. Draw up a key grid with B minor as the tonic key.
- In Bach's *Gavotte*, he modulated to the dominant key at the end of section A. Which key does he modulate to at the end of section A in the bourrée?
- The gavotte started with a characteristic two-crotchet anacrusis. How does the bourrée start?
- Which elements of this music give it a dance-like quality?

SYMPHONY NO. 41, 3RD MOVEMENT
Mozart

The dance forms used by Bach and other Baroque composers in their suites were based on national dance styles that were originally performed by country folk. Of course, the music for these country-dances would not have been performed by an orchestra, but rather on more rustic instruments, such as the fiddle and bagpipes. What Bach and his contemporaries did was to transform the country-dances into more sophisticated musical works to be played at the equally sophisticated royal and noble courts.

One of the dances that the Baroque composers included in their dance suites was the **minuet**. Later in the eighteenth century, composers working in the Classical style often included a minuet as the third movement of their symphonies. Mozart was no exception. Listen to CD 2, track 4, and you will hear the third movement of his 41st (and last) symphony.

Like the Baroque dance suite movements, this minuet is in binary form. Once again, go back to project one and remind yourself about binary form.

In the teacher's resource file there is a listening assignment for you to complete including questions to answer using a score. However, without any reference to the score, try the following tasks as you listen to Mozart's minuet.

Listening tasks

◆ This minuet is in the key of C major. Draw up a key grid with C major as the tonic key.
◆ Listen to Mozart's minuet and identify the A and B sections of the binary form.
◆ Which key does Mozart modulate to at the end of his A section?
◆ Compare and contrast the styles of the bourrée that we analysed on pages 78–80 and this minuet by Mozart. Which features of each piece identify the style of the music? Which is in the Baroque style and which is in the Classical style? How can you tell?

MORNING PAPERS
Strauss (1825–99)

Fashions change and by the early nineteenth century the minuet had become a rather archaic dance. As a musical form, it was also not so popular. In the symphony, composers were writing faster third movement pieces that they called **scherzos** and in both music and high-society dances, the minuet all but disappeared.

The minuet was replaced by a new dance that was called the **waltz**. As is so often the case, when this new dance first appeared in the dance halls of Europe, it caused quite a stir. It was not just that the waltz was more exuberant and energetic than the rather refined and gentile minuet. What caused the fuss was that the man and woman as dance partners would actually be face-to-face throughout the dance *and* they were required to hold each other closely, with their arms around each other.

The centre of waltzing was Vienna. It was reported that during the 1832 Carnival Week in Vienna, there were over 750 waltz balls held, attended by over 20,000 people (out of a total population of 40,000). The success of these balls meant that there was plenty of work for orchestral musicians and special 'waltz orchestras' were formed. One of the leaders of these orchestras was Johann Strauss who, together with his son (also Johann Strauss) composed many waltz tunes of his own.

All of these waltzes had their own titles. *Morning Papers* by Johann Strauss the younger (as the son is usually known) is a typical example. In fact, *Morning Papers* is not one waltz but several strung together as a medley. This is not unlike the way in which dance tracks are 'mixed' into each other, one after another, in the dance and club music of today.

Morning Papers starts, as was the norm, with a short introduction that, in effect, summons the dancers to their feet and tells them to prepare for dancing. To distinguish the introduction from the waltz proper, the introduction is in 2/4 time, as opposed to the 3/4 time of the waltz.

There then follows the first waltz of the medley, in 3/4 time and in ternary form, with the two main themes being played and repeated in an **A B A** pattern.

The first waltz in the medley is followed by the second waltz, which is also in ternary form. To avoid confusion we will call the two themes of this waltz **C** and **D**.

C

D

Introduction	D major
Waltz 1 – Section **A**	G major
Waltz 1 – Section **B**	D major
Waltz 1 – Section **A**	G major
Waltz 2 – Section **C**	C major
Waltz 2 – Section **D**	G major
Waltz 2 – Section **C**	C major

You will notice that as well as using contrasting melodies, Strauss also uses tonality to give shape to his composition.

The extract on CD 2, track 5, takes you as far as the second waltz in the medley. There are three more waltzes in *Morning Papers* as well as a coda at the end. If you are able to, listen to a complete recording of the whole medley. See if you can identify the keys of the third, fourth and fifth waltzes.

One of the most important figures in the history, development and promotion of English folkdance music was not the musician or dancer, but a publisher by the name of John Playford. Playford was born in Norwich in 1623 and is thought to have attended the Cathedral choir school there. However, he made his career in London as a publisher of political documents, music theory books and collections of songs and dances.

The English Dancing Master

From 1851 until his death in 1686, Playford published seven editions of a compendium of English dance tunes under the title of *The English Dance Master*. These books contained a large range of dance tunes in a variety of tempi and metres, together with instructions for the dance steps themselves. It is probable that Playford engaged a team of musicians to collate his *Dancing Master* series.

Maggots

The tunes Playford published were not new compositions, but rather traditional country dance tunes, which were transcribed for publication. These dances included the boree (the English version of the bourrée), the jig, the rigadoon and the maggot. Maggots took a variety of musical characteristics and were not tied to any particular metre or rhythmic style. However, they were always melodious and jolly affairs. In old English, the word 'maggot' was applied to something lightweight or trivial. Alternatively, it could be applied to a person of easy-going manner. Perhaps that is why many maggots were dedicated to named persons, as in *Mr Lane's Maggot*, *My Lord Byron's Maggot* and *Betty's Maggot*.

Ever since they were first published, this collection of tunes has been of central importance to English folk musicians. Listen to CD 2, track 6, which features a performance of the tune *Dick's Maggot* by the accordionist Roger Nicholls.

☀ Performance tasks

◆ In pairs, play through this arrangement of *Dick's Maggot*. As well as mastering your own individual parts, pay particular attention to the *ensemble* between the two players. The rhythmic interplay between the two parts, for example, in the very first bar, where the upper part is syncopated against the lower part, is especially important in creating the dance-like lilt of the music.

◆ When you have played these two lines as a duet, one of you should play the top line whilst the other improvises an accompaniment on a keyboard or fretboard instrument. The harmonies can be quite simple and you can work out some of them from the lower melody part. Remember that chords I, IV and V in G major are the chords of G, C and D. Stick to these three chords and you will not go far wrong – except at the end of bars 12 and 20, when the music modulates briefly to the key of D major.

◆ Try adding a simple rhythmic ostinato to accompany your duet.

In the teacher's resource file there are three more maggots for you to play and arrange: *Jack's Maggot*, *Draper's Maggot* and *Mr Beveridge's Maggot*.

THE CHARLESTON
Cecil Mack and Jimmy Johnson

The roaring twenties

The Wall Street Crash of 1929 brought great depression and hardship to many American people. In contrast, the early years of the decade were times of great fun and these years became known as the 'roaring twenties'.

Despite the prohibition of the sale and consumption of alcohol in the United States between 1920 and 1933, music and dancing were increasingly popular forms of entertainment. Much of this was due to the rise of jazz and other popular musical styles. Many new dances were invented, including the Charleston, a fast and furious dance that is reputed to have started on the dockside in the town of Charleston, South Carolina. It featured a great deal of backwards leg kicking and flapping of the arms and became very popular with young people. Young ladies who favoured this dance became known as 'flappers'.

In 1923, the hit musical *Runnin' Wild* featured a song called *The Charleston*. It was this song that propelled the dance to international popularity and a place in musical history.

Follow the lyrics as you listen to the recording of *The Charleston* on CD 2, track 7.

Carolina, Carolina, at last you're on the map.
With a new tune, funny blue tune, with a
    peculiar snap!
You may not be able to buck or wing,
    foxtrot, two-step, or even sing,
But if you ain't got religion in your feet you
    can do this dance and do it neat!

Charleston! Charleston! Made in Carolina!
Some dance, some prance, I say there's
    nothing finer than the
Charleston! Charleston! Gee, how you can
    shuffle!
Ev'ry step you do leads to something new.
    Man, I'm telling you – it's a lark!

Buck dance, wing dance, will be a back
    number, but the
Charleston! Charleston! That dance is surely
    a comer.
Sometime, you'll dance it one time,
That dance called the Charleston, made in
    South Caroline.

The main idea or 'hook' of the song features a small, characteristic syncopated motif that typifies the Charleston musical style:

Listening tasks

◆ If you study the accompaniment for these two bars, you will notice a small 'fill' that is played between the words 'Charleston! Charleston!' On the CD recording, which instruments play this fill?
◆ After *The Charleston* has been sung, the singer and the band immediately segue into another song from the 1920s called *Five Foot Two*:

Five foot two, eyes of blue,
But oh! What those five foot could do,
Has anybody seen my girl?
Turned up nose, turned down hose,
Bet ya' life she's one of those!
Has anybody seen my girl?
Silken slips, painted lips,
Covered with fur,
Diamond rings and all those things,
Betcha' life it isn't her.
But could she smooch, could she woo?
Could she, could she, could she coo?
Has anybody seen my girl?

Listen carefully to the recording and identify the musical similarities between the two songs that enable them to be segued (joined) together.

ROCK AROUND THE CLOCK
Max C. Freedman and Jimmy de Knight

Rock and roll

On 12 April 1954, a recording session took place that was to revolutionize both popular music and popular dancing. The song that was recorded was *Rock Around the Clock*, performed by Bill Haley and his Comets.

The music was not completely revolutionary – the chord structure was based around the twelve-bar blues that had been the basis of much popular and jazz music since the start of the century. The instruments played in the band had been evolving through the popular country and western styles of the 1940s, and the vocal style was tuneful and clearly pronounced. The style of dancing that went with the song (it was used as the opening music for the film *The Blackboard Jungle*) was not particularly revolutionary either, evolving as it did from the popular swing and jitterbug dance styles that accompanied big band music in the 1940s.

What was revolutionary about *Rock Around the Clock* was that it positively encouraged young people (teenagers as they became known) to go out, freely enjoy themselves and dance until they dropped. This coupled with the fast tempo of the song and the rhythmic impetus given to the music, particularly at the start of the song, made it a focus for teenage rebellion.

Listen to the opening of *Rock Around the Clock*, which is on CD 2, track 8.

> One, two, three o'clock, four o'clock, rock,
> Five, six, seven o'clock, eight o'clock, rock,
> Nine, ten, eleven o'clock, twelve o'clock, rock,
> We're gonna rock around the clock tonight.
>
> Put your glad rags on and join me, hon,
> We'll have some fun when the clock strikes one,
> We're gonna rock around the clock tonight,
> We're gonna rock, rock, rock, 'til broad daylight.
> We're gonna rock, gonna rock, around the clock tonight.

The song is in the key of A major and each verse follows the classic twelve-bar blues chord sequence (see the chart below).

Well, put your A glad rags on and	A join me, hon, We'll	A have some fun when the	A clock strikes one, We're gonna
D rock around the	D clock tonight, We're gonna	A rock, rock, rock, 'til	A broad daylight, We're gonna rock
E gonna rock, around	E the clock tonight.	A	A

Listening tasks

◆ Listen carefully to the bass line played by the double bass. How are the notes played by the double bass selected?

◆ What is noticeable about the rhythm of the bass line?

◆ The introduction to the song ('One, two, three o'clock, four o'clock, rock') clearly adds to the sense of anticipation and excitement created by the song. How does the music help to create this mood? In your answer, refer to the way that the melody line is built up, the way in which the backing instruments are used and the way that musical motifs are repeated and developed.

◆ How are the melody notes for the verses worked out? Are there any links between the vocal melody line and the double bass line?

The Blackboard Jungle

The 1955 release of *The Blackboard Jungle*, the film for which *Rock Around the Clock* provided the title music, was itself a key event in the development of a teenage culture. The film is about a middle-aged teacher who is set to work in a tough city high school where the teenage students make the rules and the staff weakly accept the fact that they have lost control.

When the teacher tries exerting his authority, he receives much hostility from both students and some of his colleagues, culminating in a threat delivered to his pregnant wife. In anger, the teacher hurls an accusation at Gregory Miller, a student whom he suspects of being the chief troublemaker in his class.

The moral message of the film centres on this accusation, alongside the issues of control, authority, prejudice and inner-city deprivation. In 1955 this film and its message, coupled with the music of *Rock Around the Clock*, had an incredible impact. Some people might say that things have never been the same since.

STAYIN' ALIVE
Barry, Robin and Maurice Gibb

Saturday night fever

In much the same way that the rock and roll revolution was catapulted to public attention through the release of a film, it was the 1978 film *Saturday Night Fever* that turned disco into a worldwide phenomenon. Disco had evolved throughout the 1970s, bringing together technological developments in sound systems and lighting, as well as outrageous fashions in clothing.

Musically, the disco style brought together a variety of dance styles, including Latin rhythms, and the vocal styles of soul music. There was a rich quality to the instrumental accompaniments of 1970s disco songs, too, with the use of 'live' orchestral backing tracks alongside the use of the full range of electric guitars and drums.

Listen to CD 2, track 9, which is the opening of the song *Stayin' Alive* from *Saturday Night Fever*. The brothers Barry, Robin and Maurice Gibb, better known as The Bee Gees, composed the song and it is The Bee Gees who perform the song here.

Well, you can tell by the way by the way I
*   use my walk,*
I'm a woman's man: no time to talk.
Music loud and women warm.
I've been kicked around since I was born.
And now it's all right, it's OK,
And you may look the other way.
We can try to understand the New York
*   Times' effect on man.*
Whether you're a brother or whether
*   you're a mother,*
You're stayin' alive, stayin' alive.
Feel the city breakin' and ev'rybody shakin'
And we're stayin' alive, stayin' alive.
Ah, ha, ha, ha, stayin' alive, stayin' alive.
Ah, ha, ha, ha, stayin' alive.

This song is typical of the 1970s disco musical style. This style is founded on a simple yet distinctive basic drum pattern within each four-beat bar.

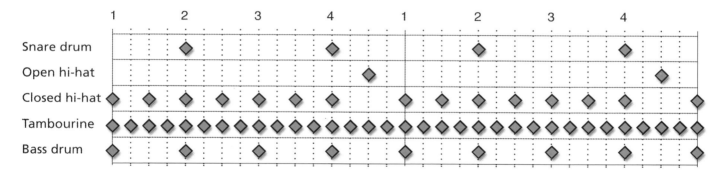

This pattern is very repetitive, with the tambourine playing continuous semiquavers, the bass drum playing on every beat, the snare drum playing on every other beat and the hi-hat cymbal playing on every quaver. Note that the open hi-hat plays on the seventh quaver of every bar, with the closed hi-hat being played on every other quaver.

The guitar parts in the accompaniment are repetitive, too, but they are also more complex rhythmically.

The rhythm guitar plays a continuous semiquaver 'block' chord pattern. This is given a distinctive sound through the use of a 'wah-wah' pedal and very fast, light strokes across the guitar strings. The lead guitar plays an equally distinctive and repetitive riff that uses syncopated, funky rhythms. The bass guitar line also uses the same syncopated, funky rhythms and at some points the bass and lead guitars are doubling each other.

Finally, you cannot fail to notice the distinctive vocal performance of The Bee Gees. As well as their use of the falsetto range and their individual vocal accents (the brothers Gibb were originally from Manchester, grew up in Australia, and recorded the music for *Saturday Night Fever* in the United States), listen carefully for their precise close harmony work and their use of parallel vocal harmonies. Listen too for the orchestral strings as a 'pad' to weld all of the complex rhythms together.

Garage

Garage is one of the various varieties of dance music popular on the club scene at the start of the twentieth-first century. Garage has its roots in the music first put together by the DJ Larry Levan at the Paradise Garage Nightclub in New York. Levan gained a reputation for mixing together sounds from classic 1970s disco tracks, sampled electronic sounds and funky rock records. What resulted was a sound clearly based on the 70s disco sound, but with heavier, funkier bass lines and a contemporary edge provided by the electronic samples.

Craig David

Craig David is probably best known for his collaboration with The Artful Dodger on the hit song *Rewind*. He has also enjoyed a number of solo successes, including the single *Fill Me In*, which reached the number one spot when Craig was only 19 years old, making him one of the youngest solo male singers to reach the top spot in the charts.

Craig David's music is clearly in the Garage tradition, with meticulously crafted rhythm and bass lines and extremely clever use of samples. However, Craig is more than merely a recording artist. He is equally at home performing live and has given acoustic performances of his songs, with an acoustic guitar accompaniment, in concert and on television. He has also co-hosted (with Mark Hill of The Artful Dodger) a Garage show on London's Capital radio as well as MC-ing and DJ-ing in London and Southampton.

Inter selecta
Hyper, hyper, hyper, that's what we make ya/Time to mash up the speaker/
Craig David, Artful Dodger/Inter selecta (x4)
Making moves yeah on the dance floor/Got our groove on dancing yeah real hardcore/
From the front to the back that's where I was at/You know, you know, the Artful Dodger do it like that/With Craig David all over your .../DJ it's all up to you/When the crowd go wild/Tell me, whatcha gon' do.

Re-e wind/When the crowd say bo selecta/Re-e-e-e-e-e-wind/When the crowd say bo selecta-ta/Re-e-wind/When the crowd say bo selecta/Re-e-e-e-e-e-wind/When the crowd say bo, bo, bo/Re-e-wind/When the crowd say bo selecta/Re-e-e-e-e-wind/When the crowd say bo selecta-ta/Re-e-e-wind/When the crowd say bo selecta/Re-e-e-e-e-wind/This goes out to all the DJs.

Eh, yeah/Eh, eh yeah (yeah)(x3)/Eh, yeah/Eh (yeah)

Listening tasks

- Listen to the recording of *Rewind* by The Artful Dodger, featuring Craig David, on CD 2, track 10.
- Describe the vocal styles of the introduction to this song. How is technology used to enhance the voices?
- One of the most memorable things about this song is the way that the voice samples are used. Describe how the voice samples have been made and used.
- Comment on the pitch range of the vocal solos that are sung by Craig David.
- How are the percussion instruments used in this song?
- What other percussive sounds are used in this song? How are these sounds used and how effective are they?
- The bass line and other instrumental parts for this song are quite minimal. What effect does this have on the song as a whole?
- Is this good music for dancing to? Give reasons for your answer.

MUSIC FROM INDIA

A great big melting pot

The world is getting smaller. Not literally, but the ever increasing development of technology and communications, such as satellites and the Internet, mean that it is now easier than ever before to communicate with and learn from different cultures.

In music, this means that we are able to listen to and analyse many different styles and flavours of music from every corner of the globe through the World Wide Web, through radio and through digitally recorded sound. This is good news as it means it is far easier for us to gain an appreciation and an understanding of music from different cultures other than our own.

This has led to a fascinating cross-fertilization of musical cultures, where composers from one culture have listened to music from another culture and have then incorporated music from that other culture into their own compositional style. This multi-influenced music is known as **fusion**.

Indian classical music

In the same way that we study, analyse and perform western Classical music, the study and performance of Indian Classical music is a serious and distinguished art form. In fact, the spirituality, ritual and tradition that pervade every aspect of Indian music make it more of a way of life than art form.

Central to the tradition and ritual of Indian music is the role of the music teacher, who is a revered and honoured member of the community and not just as a musician, but also as a spiritual leader.

Structurally, Indian Classical music is very similar to western Classical music in that it is built on three main elements: harmony, melody and rhythm.

Drones for harmony

The basis of all harmony in Indian music is the **drone**. As in western Classical music, the drone is a constant, repeating note, usually in the bass, over which melodies and other harmonies move. Usually, the drone is played on a low-pitched string instrument called the **tambura**. When giving a musical performance, it is usual for the teacher to grant the 'privilege' of playing the accompanying drone on the tambura to the most advanced student in the class.

The drone usually consists of two different pitches, what we would call the tonic of the piece (the note around which the melody centres and returns to), and the note a fourth or fifth above that 'tonic'.

Taals for rhythm

Every composition in Indian Classical music is built around a **taal**. A taal is a short, basic, rhythmic phrase that is repeated over and over again throughout the piece, in much the same way that some western Classical music is built around a rhythmic ostinato – Ravel's *Bolero* is an obvious example.

However, unlike the snare drum ostinato in *Bolero*, a taal does not merely repeat, unchanged, throughout the piece. Whilst all this is going on, a constant beat is maintained. This beat is called the **matras**. Over this matra goes a set of rhythmic patterns known as **bols**.

The matras and bols are played on the **tabla**, a set of two small drums that are hand-held and hand-played. Like the notes of the drone, one of the drums in the tabla is tuned to the tonic of the piece being played, whilst the other drum is tuned to the dominant or subdominant note.

Raags for melody

Like western Classical music, the melodies of Indian Classical music are built on a system of scales. In the same way that western musicians use major and minor scales, Indian musicians use **raags**. However, unlike western music where the number of major scales is restricted to twelve, with enharmonic equivalents (equal to the number of notes in the chromatic spectrum), there are over 200 raags in the Indian Classical tradition. Whereas every major scale in western musical culture is built in exactly the same pattern of tones and semitones, every raag is built in a different way.

Raags are much more than scales of notes, though. As well as being constructed in a unique way, every raag is associated with a particular time of day, a particular season of the year, and a particular emotion or feeling. Remember that Indian Classical music has an important spiritual dimension as well as strict musical structures.

Some raags contain just five notes – what western musicians would call **pentatonic**. However, there is no fixed rule as to how many notes can or should be in a raag as each one is different. The player of the main melody instrument in a composition uses the raag as the basis for improvisation. Usually, and significantly, this player will be the revered teacher and spiritual leader.

The best-known melody instrument is the **sitar** and other melody instruments include the **surbahar** (a bass version of the sitar) and the **sarangi** (another string instrument that is played with a bow, unlike the sitar and the surbahar, which are both plucked).

Raag Bhoplal

Listen to CD 2, track 11, which features a performance of the *Raag Bhoplal*. On this recording, the sitar is played by the virtuoso musician Irshad Khan. He is accompanied in the traditional manner by his pupil Surjit Sen, who plays a drone accompaniment on the tambura, and by the master tabla player Vineet Vyas.

The *Raag Bhoplal* is a raag to be played at night-time and is associated with harmony and contentment. It is also a raag that is easily identifiable and approachable for western musical ears, as it is a pentatonic raag.

The strings of the melody instrument are tuned to the familiar pentatonic scale:

Listening tasks

- Listen to the recording and identify the main features of the Indian musical style (drone, taal and raag) that have been described.
- Look at the notes in the raag and then listen to the drone that is played on the tambura. Which notes are played in the drone?
- How does the taal develop during the extract on the CD?

Raag Bilaskhani Todi

Listen to CD 2, track 12. This music is based on the *Raag Bilaskhani Todi*, an early morning raag that is also associated with sorrow and grief.

The performers are the table player Anindo Chatterjee, an unknown tambura player, and the vocalist Sulochana Brahaspati. The vocal style, which, like the sitar playing in the *Raag Bhoplal*, is largely improvised, is in the **khyal** style. Khyal is highly melismatic and ornamented.

Listening tasks

- Which is the more expressive of the two raags that you have listened to: the *Raag Bhoplal* or the *Raag Bilaskhani Todi*? Give musical reasons for your choice.

RAHAYE, RAHAYE; NUKHE CHAKEE JAVANA; AAG

The Safri Boys; Achanak; C.I.D.

Bhangra beatz

The original **bhangra** was a style of folk music sung and played by agricultural workers in the northern Indian province of the Punjab. However, over the past 30 years, the term bhangra has been associated with an exciting fusion of traditional Indian musical styles with western popular music styles.

Western pop music has developed in many and diverse ways over the past 30 years. If you make a list of all the different pop styles that you can think of from the past 30 years you will get some kind of idea. Likewise, bhangra is not one particular style, but rather a large range of fusion styles that have evolved alongside western popular styles. Bhangra is fundamentally a British phenomenon, drawing on the rich traditions of second and third generation British-Asian families and the traditions of the British pop music industry.

On CD 2, tracks 13, 14 and 15, you can hear three examples of bhangra music.

The first track, *Rahaye, Rahaye*, is by The Safri Boys. Listen particularly for the melodic style of the vocalist. You will hear similarities with the khyal vocal style shown in the *Raag Bilaskhani Todi*.

The second track, *Nukhe Chakee Javana* by Achanak, is heavily in the contemporary rhythm and blues style with references to rap, khyal vocalizing, the use of samples and scratching. The track also features use of both the English and Punjabi languages.

The third track, *Aag* by C.I.D. (Commercial Indian Dance), is a fusion of Indian music styles and contemporary house/dance music. Listen particularly for the opening drum rhythm, reminiscent of the taal style, and the heavy bass drone that underpins the harmony of the track.

Salsa style

Like the spicy tomato that shares its name, salsa is an exciting blend of musical flavours that come together to form a distinctive experience. Musically, salsa is a generic term given to the wide range of Latin-American dance music. The origins of the authentic salsa sound are in the dance and vocal folk music of Cuba and the big band jazz of the United States and in particular, New York.

 ## Cuban history

The island of Cuba has a fascinating history. Today we know Cuba as the island that became a communist state after the revolution of 1959, with its enigmatic leader Fidel Castro. Before this, Cuba had spent time as a Spanish colony and had played a large part in the slave trade from Africa. All of this has led to Cuba developing an extremely rich, varied and complex cultural identity. Musically, this includes strong Spanish and Latin influences, flavours of African culture (particularly from the West coast of Africa, where most of the slaves had come from), together with a lively, vital approach to the arts in general that has undoubtedly been developed through the years of colonial rule and the years of communist rule.

The roots of salsa

There are two forms of indigenous Cuban music that are important to the development of salsa. The first is the **rumba**, which is not a stylized dance (as you might see in western ballroom dancing), but rather a whole dance tradition. Rumba dances can be fast or slow, to be danced by couples, by groups of people or by solo male dancers. Musically, rumba dance styles are built on a battery of percussion sounds and the most important central percussionist is the player of the claves. The word 'claves' literally means 'key' and the initial rhythm played by the claves player holds the key to the tempo and style of the rumba dance about to be performed.

The second form, where there is singing with the dance music, the rumba might be known as a **son** (song). Again, in a son, the percussion section is very important with the claves player holding the key role. Other percussion instruments used in the rumba and the son include the maracas, the guiro and the timbales (resonant, almost-pitched drums played with a hard stick).

With the revolution of 1959, a number of Cuba's most popular musicians left the island and headed for New York. There, they encountered many new forms of music including jazz and, in particular, big band jazz. Inevitably, the indigenous music that the Cuban musicians brought with them to New York began to cross-fertilize with the jazz styles and salsa was born.

Listen to CD 2, track 16. The recording is of the song *Bamboleo*, performed by the singer who has been dubbed 'The Queen of Salsa', Celia Cruz, accompanied by The Fania All Stars. 'Fania' is a New York recording label founded in the 1960s specifically to record salsa music and The Fania All Stars were the 'house' band put together by the record company. In time, the band developed into a collection of the very best salsa solo instrumentalists who, as well as recording their own albums, would come together from time to time to give live concerts and back great vocalists, such as Celia Cruz.

Most salsa tunes follow a set formal pattern that is derived from the forms of rumba and son. The piece begins with a short instrumental introduction, usually featuring repeated or riff patterns from the **orquestra** (as salsa bands are known). The vocal soloist then enters over a reduced band, mainly percussion, usually singing in free time or performing an **inspiracione** (improvisation). Then the chorus is heard, where the solo singer is sometimes joined by a group of backing singers. Sometimes the solo and backing singers perform in a call and response pattern.

Listen to *Bamboleo* and follow through the sections of
the song – the opening riff, the inspiracione and the
chorus. This performance is in the key of F minor. Here
is the orquestra riff that opens the song:

You might want to sing along to the extremely catchy
chorus section:

However, it might be a challenge for you to match the
vocal dexterity and the rhythmic precision of Celia Cruz
during her inspiracione at the beginning of the song.

On the CD-ROM that accompanies *Heinemann GCSE
Music*, there is a sequenced version of the orquestra riff
and the chorus sections of *Bamboleo* for you to use as
the basis for your own arrangement or your own
composition in the salsa style.

To twenty-first century musicians in the West, the sound of the Javanese and Balinese **gamelan** is instantly recognizable, but like so many musical traditions from around the world, it was only the development of recording technology at the start of the twentieth century that brought this exciting music to musicians outside of Indonesia.

About gamelan

Gamelan is the name given to a musical played by an orchestra composed primarily of percussion. In Bali, gamelan orchestras consist of horizontally lying tuned gongs (known collectively as trompong), bronze suspended gongs, bronze metallophones (the gangsas), bamboo xylophones, drums (the kempur), fiddles (the rehabs) and flutes (sulings). Gamelan music is, like Indian music, constructed using a unique system of scales. The most common types of scale used in the gamelan are the pentatonic (five-note) scale, known as **sléndro**, and the heptatonic (seven-note) scale, known as **pélog**.

Gamelan music is functional in that the music is played to accompany particular occasions, such as public ceremonies (weddings, funerals and coronations), or public entertainments that combine several arts, such as drama and dance.

Textures of gamelan

The texture of Balinese gamelan music is characterized by two elements. Firstly, the music is full of evolving ostinati patterns, that is, repeated rhythmic and melodic motifs that, over time, gradually change their shape and character. Secondly, gamelan music is built from individual, seemingly independent, melodic lines that interlock with each other in rhythmic combat. This sort of texture is known as **heterophony**.

The simplest sort of gamelan texture has just two parts that, whilst independent, also interlock with each other. This two-part texture is known as **kotèkan**. Balinese musicians regard these two interlocking parts as being 'male' and 'female'. They are known as **sangsih** (male part) and **polos** (female part). Rhythmically, the polos line is on the beat and simpler in style, whilst the **sangsih** is off the beat and more complex in style.

Listen to CD 2, track 17, which features a recording of a Balinese gamelan orchestra, recorded in 1928 by the composer Colin McPhee. You should be able to hear the two lines of the gamelan texture, the sangsih and polos, as they play against and with each other. You should also be able to hear the pentatonic scale around which this piece is based. The stave bellows gives an approximate representation of the sléndro, although the tuning utilized by Balinese musicians is not the same as the Western tuning.

Since gamelan music was first brought to the attention and knowledge of Western musicians, many Western composers have been influenced by, or have adopted, aspects of gamelan textures into their own compositions. In particular, minimalist composers of the late twentieth century, such as Philip Glass and Steve Reich, use similar techniques of evolving ostinati and heterophonic patterns in their music. Listen to the recording of Philip Glass' *Lightning* on CD 2, track 41, read the commentary on page 147 of this book, and compare the two styles.

Jamaican music and reggae

If you mention Jamaican music in conversation, the odds are that most people will think of reggae and Bob Marley. However, the Caribbean island of Jamaica has a rich and varied musical tradition that goes back over many centuries. There are many parallels between the development of reggae out of African, Latin American and indigenous Jamaican musical styles and the development of salsa out of African, Latin American and indigenous Cuban musical styles. Like salsa, reggae has only been around for about 40 years.

In the early days of Jamaica's populated history, in the late fifteenth century, the island was occupied by the Spanish and British who imported a large number of Ghanaian slaves from Africa. Working on the many island plantations and with the benefit of their own African musical heritage, as well as the western musical heritage brought to the island by the Spanish and British, a rich folk music tradition was developed by the now native Jamaicans. One strand of this musical tradition is **mento**, a song style which, much like the tradition of **calypso** in the neighbouring island of Trinidad, is highly rhythmic in a fast and sometimes furious dance style and often contained witty, ironic lyrics with a political or sexual message. Musically, mento is characterized by an offbeat guitar 'shuffle' and this guitar style was important in the development of reggae.

Carnivals in Jamaica

The other musical tradition is **Jonkonnu**. Jonkonnu is carnival time in Jamaica and takes place in the Christmas season. Like other Caribbean carnival traditions, such as that of the US Virgin Islands, featured on page 56, Jonkonnu features colourful marches with the revellers dressed up as animals, kings and queens or even the devil. There is much music to accompany the marches and much of this music is improvised using a battery of percussion instruments and homemade instruments.

Religious influences and the Rastafari

Throughout Jamaica's history, religion has always played an important part in everyday life. The Spanish and British colonialists converted many of the former African slaves to Christianity. However, some of them developed a new religion that had, at its heart, a belief that one day they will return to Africa, which they refer to as 'Zion', and that the late Emperor of Ethiopia, Haile Selasse I, was and still is the prince of the Rastafari. Rastafarians preach peace and love and they believe in the equal worth of every person, so long as that person believes in Jah, the spirit of God, and they sacramentally smoke cannabis (ganja) as their holy herb.

Rock steady and reggae roots

It is from this colourful, cultural background that reggae emerged in the early 1960s. At the end of World War II, technological advances and relatively increased prosperity meant that radio sets and record players became available in Jamaica on a wide scale. This meant that native Jamaicans were able to hear jazz and rock and roll music from the United States in addition to their own folk music traditions of mento and Jonkonnu. The rest is history. American and Jamaican styles cross-fertilized and in the 1950s, a new style of music was born.

Rock steady was a lively mix of mento/Jonkonnu offbeat chords and dance rhythms, together with the harmonic and riff-based structures of American popular music. As this music was developed and became more sophisticated (and commercial), the style became known as **ska** (after the skank, an off-beat dance that accompanied the rock steady tunes), and finally, reggae.

The rudeboys

After the independence celebrations of 1962, there was a massive expansion of the Jamaican capital, Kingston. This led to the development of poor districts known as shantytowns, such as Trenchtown and Dungle. In these areas there was unemployment, crime and abuse, and it was from these areas that a group of angry, sometimes lawless and violent, young men emerged. Known as the **rudeboys**, their adoption of the reggae style and culture brought a new dimension to reggae lyric writing.

Desmond Dekker

Born in Kingston in 1942, Desmond Dekker was one of the first great stars of reggae and was certainly one of the first reggae singers to achieve international recognition. His song *The Israelites*, which dates from 1969, has all the classical musical features of reggae. It is based in the philosophy of the Rastafarian religion and also highlights the plight of the poor and the rudeboys in Kingston's shantytowns. Dekker was an orphan who worked as a welder before he gained international recognition as a musician.

Listen to CD 2, track 18, which features Desmond Dekker singing *The Israelites*.

> *Get up in the morning, slaving for bread, sir,*
> *So that every mouth can be fed.*
> *Oh, oh, me Israelites.*
>
> *My wife and my kids they pack-up-and-leave*
> *   me,*
> *Dahlin', she said, I was yours to receive.*
> *Oh, oh, me Israelites.*
>
> *Shirt them-a-tear-up-trousers and go,*
> *I don't want to end up like Bonnie and*
> *   Clyde,*
> *Oh, oh, me Israelites.*
>
> *After a storm there must be a calm,*
> *If you catch me on the farm, you sound your*
> *   alarm,*
> *Oh, oh, me Israelites.*

Here is the vocal melody for the first verse.

Notice three things about this vocal melody. Firstly, it is syncopated. This is important when you listen to the melody against the steady offbeat chordal accompaniment. Secondly, notice the way that the entire melody centres (and always returns to) the tonic note of B flat. Lastly, note how Desmond Dekker has used the arpeggio of B flat major in the central part of the melody. Again, if you look at the bass line, you will see similar arpeggio patterns.

Now listen for the guitar accompaniment that is heard throughout the song.

Notice the way that the chords are all played on the off beats, for example the second and fourth beats in every bar. The chords used are the standard primary chords in B flat major (B flat, E flat and F – chords I, IV and V), with the addition of the surprise chord of G flat in the final bar of the sequence. This chord pattern is repeated consistently throughout the song.

Now listen to the bass line for this song.

You will notice that the bass line is centred round the arpeggio of the chord being played at that time. The exception to this rule is the final bar of the sequence, where a scale of G flat major is played.

Now listen to the rhythm track of this song. The drum grid below represents the type of rhythm tracks played in reggae.

Notice there is heavy emphasis given to the second and fourth beats of the bars, as there was with the chord parts. This is known as the reggae 'one drop' rhythmic style, with the first and third beats of the bar being effectively 'dropped' by the heaviest percussion instruments.

Performance tasks

◆ Use the information and score extracts given to you here to make an ensemble performance of *The Israelites*. If your ensemble includes orchestral instruments, think how you might best employ them to play the chord, bass or rhythm lines. Use the recording on CD 2, track 18 to guide your arrangement.

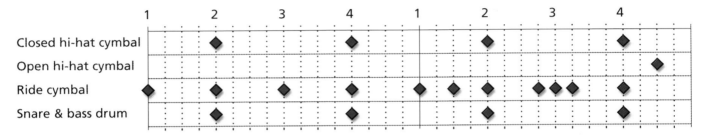

LIPH'IQINISO
Ladysmith Black Mambazo

The spirit of South Africa

The advances in technology over the past 50 years (recording on tape, vinyl and CD, the boom in television and radio and the Internet), has meant that we have been able to access almost every style and tradition of music from the comfort of our own homes. This has been marvellous in terms of increasing education and understanding about music, but there has been a rather paradoxical knock-on effect that, in view of some people, some aspects of the world's musical heritage are being destroyed.

The problem is this. If you are a composer, your own individual compositional style will be influenced by your own, personal musical experiences. This has always been the case; even Bach and Mozart were influenced in their own writing by other composers. In the case of world music composers, this can be very exciting, as we have seen with salsa, where Cuban son merges with American jazz, and reggae, where Jamaican mento merges with American rock and roll. However, it could also mean that these distinctive, unique musical styles could eventually be submerged into one, universal, global music style, which economists and environmental protesters often refer to as 'globalization'.

To counter this threat of musical globalization, several musical groups have worked tirelessly to protect and promote the musical traditions of their native countries. Possibly the most successful of these groups is the South African vocal group Ladysmith Black Mambazo. The story of the group's rise to fame and the music that they perform is told on their own website, www.mambazo.com.

Ladysmith Black Mambazo

Listen to CD 2, track 19. The recording features Ladysmith Black Mambazo singing the traditional African song *Liph'Iqiniso*.

Ladysmith Black Mambazo have come to represent the traditional culture of South Africa. They are regarded as South Africa's cultural emissaries at home and around the world. In 1993, at Nelson Mandela's request, Ladysmith Black Mambazo accompanied the future President, and then South African President F.W. de Klerk, to the Nobel Peace Prize ceremony in Oslo, Norway. They also sang at President Mandela's inauguration in May 1994. They are a national treasure of the new South Africa in part because they embody the traditions suppressed in the old South Africa.

The traditional music sung by Ladysmith Black Mambazo is called isicathamiya (is-cot-a-me-ya). It was born in the mines of South Africa. Black workers were taken by rail to work far away from their homes and their families. Poorly housed and paid worse, they would entertain themselves after a six-day week by singing songs into the small hours every Sunday morning. 'Cothoza Mfana' they called themselves, 'tip toe guys', referring to the dance steps choreographed so as not to disturb the camp security guards.

When miners returned to the homelands, the tradition returned with them. There began a fierce but social competition held regularly and a highlight of everyone's social calendar. The winners were awarded a goat for their efforts and the adoration of their fans. These competitions are held even today in YMCA assembly halls and church basements throughout 'Zululand'.

In the mid 1950s, Joseph Shabalala took advantage of his proximity to the urban sprawl of the city of Durban, allowing him the opportunity to seek work in a factory. Leaving the family farm was not easy, but it was during this time that Joseph first showed a talent for singing. After singing with a few groups in Durban, he returned to his hometown of Ladysmith and began to put together groups of his own. He was rarely satisfied with the results.

'I felt there was something missing ... I tried to teach the music that I felt, but I failed, until 1964, when a dream came to me. I always hear the harmony from that dream and I said, "This is the harmony that I want and I can teach it to my guys." '

Joseph recruited members of his immediate family, brothers Headman and Jockey, cousins Albert and Abednego Mazibuko and other close friends to join. Joseph taught the group the harmonies from his dreams. With time and patience, Joseph's work began to reveal the colours of these dreams.

The name 'Ladysmith Black Mambazo' came about as a result of winning every singing competition in which the group entered. 'Ladysmith' is the hometown of the Shabalala family; 'Black' makes reference to black oxen, considered to be the strongest animal on the farm. The Zulu word 'Mambazo' refers to an axe, symbolic of the groups' ability to 'chop down' the competition. So good were they that after a time they were forbidden to enter the competitions, but welcomed instead to entertain at them.

Listening tasks

◆ The vocal textures in this piece are call and response. The calls are monophonic and the responses are homophonic. What is meant by the terms 'call and response', 'monophonic' and 'homophonic'?
◆ This music is *a cappella*. What does this term mean and what does the term mean literally?
◆ Describe two types of body music used by the singers to accompany the singing.
◆ What are the vocal ranges of the singers featured in this performance?

Thomas Mapfumo

Thomas Mapfumo is probably the most celebrated musician to have emerged from Zimbabwe since the country became independent in 1980. Mapfumo (or 'TM' as he is more usually known) is famous for his compositions that bring together and fuse the traditional instruments and rhythmic patterns of Zimbabwean music and the chord structures, instrumental riffs and even the electronic resources of western pop music. His music, like western pop music, is commercial and sometimes heavily studio-produced but, at the same time, his music never loses the raw and vital edge of the Zimbabwean roots. There is great energy in his music, which certainly lives up to the name of Zimbabwe's capital, Harare (which, literally translated, means 'don't stop').

One of the native Zimbabwean musical instruments that TM uses in his compositions is the **mbira**, a tuned percussion instrument that consists of a number of tuned metal splints that are depressed and then released to give a vibrating 'twang'. The mbira is sometimes called a 'thumb piano'. The music played by this instrument is extremely powerful and reverberant and fits well with western pop music timbres.

Chimurenga challenge

During the struggles for Zimbabwean independence in the 1970s, TM developed a style of music that became known as **chimurenga**, or 'liberation war' music. This infectious, inspiring music became a focal point for many of the oppressed black communities in Zimbabwe and the songs were in the Shona and Ndebebe languages, which could not be understood by the white colonists who ruled Zimbabwe (or Rhodesia, as it was formerly known). Many of the lyrics contained overt or subtle political messages.

Listen to CD 2, track 20, which features an extract from Thomas Mapfumo's song *Ngoma Yekwedu*. On the CD, Thomas Mapfumo and The Blacks Unlimited, a Zimbabwean instrumental and vocal group, perform the song.

Listen carefully to the recording, making special notes of the following musical features:

◆ The 'non-stop' rhythm track provided by a very light and agile hi-hat cymbal (from western pop music), the **axatse** (African shaker) and the hand hit congas.
◆ The call and response vocal textures that are so typical of African vocal music.
◆ The resonant **mbira** line that is also doubled on the electric (lead) guitar (another instrument that has a powerful, resonating tone) and the organ.

THE VOICE
Brendan Graham

The Celtic wind

Eire and the UK both have rich traditions of folk song and dance and it would be wrong to complete our exploration of world music without reference to the culture and heritage of our own area of the world.

As in Jamaica, the Punjab, Cuba and South Africa, music has always played a central role in the lives of Irish communities, both in the cities and in the country. Dance music is a central part of any Irish gathering, be it a wedding, a birthday or a wake held after a funeral. Above anything else, Irish folk music is all about participation; everyone is expected to take part, either as a performer or as a dancer. The most popular and well-known types of Irish dance tune are the **reel**, a dance in 4/4 time, and the **jig**, a dance in 6/8 time. There is even a variation on the jig called the **slip-jig**, which is in 9/8 time.

Irish instruments

The instruments commonly used in Irish folk music are the harp (not the large instruments seen at orchestral concerts, but smaller, portable hand-held versions), the wooden flute or whistle, the fiddle and the bodhrán. The bodhrán is a shallow hand-held drum, not dissimilar in shape to a tambourine, but considerably larger. It is usually played with a double-headed stick. Irish folk music also uses the uilleann pipes (as opposed to the Scottish bagpipes). They are widely used in folk bands, such as The Chieftains, and the word 'uilleann' means 'elbow'.

As with salsa and reggae, in the past 30 years traditional Irish folk music has fused with popular and rock music styles to produce a distinctive folk-rock sound. Exponents of this Irish folk-rock style include the group Clannad (originally fronted for a short time by Enya, but then replaced with her sister Máire Brennan) and The Pogues, who merged elements of the Irish folk music style with elements of punk rock in the early 1980s.

Listen to CD 2, track 21, which features a recording of the song *The Voice*, performed by Eimear Quinn. The song, which dates from 1996, combines elements of the Irish folk music style with contemporary synthesized sounds.

> *I hear your voice on the wind*
> *And I hear you call out my name.*
>
> *Listen my child, you say to me,*
> *I am the voice of your history.*
> *Be not afraid – come follow me,*
> *Answer my call and I'll set you free.*
>
> *I am the voice in the wind and the pouring rain,*
> *I am the voice of your hunger and pain,*
> *I am the voice that always is calling you,*
> *I am the voice and I will remain.*

Listening tasks

◆ Follow through the words as you listen to the recording. Which traditional Irish instruments can you hear being played and where do they enter the musical texture?

◆ How does the way in which the first two lines are set to music help to paint the meaning of those words?

◆ Is this music in a major key, a minor key, or is it modal?

A folk song from Somerset

At the start of the twentieth century, there was a great interest and revival in English folk music. Armed with reams of manuscript paper and the latest new wax-cylinder recording equipment, scholars and composers, such as Cecil Sharp and Ralph Vaughan Williams, went out on location in rural England and set about recording and notating songs and dances that had been passed from generation to generation and were part of England's rich cultural heritage.

In his original compositions, Vaughan Williams often used elements of the English folk style or even made arrangements of the songs and dances. Such was the case with his *English Folk Song Suite*. The third and final movement of this suite features several folk songs from the county of Somerset, including the well-known song *Blow Away the Morning Dew*, which is featured on CD 2, track 22.

Here is a piano reduction of Vaughan Williams' arrangement of the song:

Listening tasks

◆ Follow through both scores and identify where and how Vaughan Williams' arrangement differs from the version of the song printed on page 105.

◆ Using the piano reduction score as your guide, map out Vaughan Williams' orchestration. Annotate your score using coloured highlighter pens for each instrument (providing this is your own copy of the book).

◆ Make your own arrangements of *Blow Away the Morning Dew*, using the two scores provided here for guidance. Which of the two keys used here is best suited to your voices/instruments? Why?

BLUE SUEDE SHOES
Carl Perkins

On page 87, we looked at the first great rock and roll song, *Rock Around the Clock*. In 1956, two years after *Rock Around the Clock* was recorded, the American musician Carl Perkins composed and recorded his song *Blue Suede Shoes*. Like *Rock Around the Clock*, Perkins' song encapsulated the arrogant, almost aggressive tone and culture of the new American teenager. The song was also based on the twelve bar blues chord sequence, featured the characteristic 'walking bass' and was even in the same key of A major. The 'blue suede shoes' referred to in the song were symbols of the teenage

obsession with fashion and image. Perhaps today's teenagers might sing 'you can do anything, but don't step on my Nike trainers'.

Listen to CD 2, track 23, and use the following parts to arrange your own performance of *Blue Suede Shoes*. This version has been transposed down a third to F major, for vocal comfort. Just the basic chords are given for the accompanying instruments, which might be keyboard or guitars.

Chords

Vocals

Walking bass

Rhythm

The rhythm style for this song is the 'shuffle' style, with each beat of the 4/4 bar being divided into quaver triplets by the hi-hat cymbal. Use this rhythm as the basis for your rhythmic track.

Hi-hat cymbal
Snare drum
Bass drum

Whether you are using a 'live' drummer, a drum machine or a pre-set keyboard rhythm, you should try to vary this pattern by using fill-ins at the end of phrases. If you study the chord and walking bass parts, you will also see that at the start of each verse there are moments when the other instruments only play on the first and last beats of each bar, leaving the singer alone in the middle of each bar. Work with the keyboard player/guitarist and bass player as a unit to make this opening accompaniment really tight and punchy.

Finally, when you have given your performance, you might like to compare your interpretation with the original by Carl Perkins or the arguably more famous cover version by Elvis Presley.

MIDNIGHT TRAIN TO GEORGIA
Jim Weatherley

Sweet soul music

Soul as a recognized genre of popular music dates from the late 1950s and early 1960s. In fact, at about the same time that the salsa and reggae styles emerged. Like salsa and reggae, soul is a fusion of traditional and popular musical styles.

Many of the earliest exponents of the soul style had roots and a musical upbringing in the tradition of Gospel singing, with its characteristic call and response vocal textures. And, of course, these vocal textures were in turn derived from the traditional African vocal music that had been imported into America by the slave workers back in the eighteenth century.

When the Gospel style combined with rock and roll and swing jazz in the 1950s, a powerful musical style was created. That it was called 'soul' was no coincidence, after all, Gospel music was all about the saving of souls, too. However, it soon became clear that this kind of soul was less about spiritual matters and more about human emotions, as most of the songs dealt with the pain of love and were, sometimes, quite sexually explicit.

During the 1960s, several important sub-styles of soul developed, including Motown and Atlantic soul. The music from this period was characterized by a strong rhythmic drive, simple but strong harmonies, and often lush, colourful orchestral backings. Then there was the singing – powerful, expressive soloists backed by tight, close harmony backing vocalists (**bvox singers**) in the traditional call and response pattern.

Listen to CD 2, track 24, which features a recording of the classic soul song *Midnight Train to Georgia*, performed by the soul singer Gladys Knight.

LA proved too much for the man,
So he's leavin' the life he's come to know,
He said he's goin' back to find
Ooh, what's left of his world.
The world he left behind
Not so long ago.
He's leaving,
On that midnight train to Georgia,
And he's goin' back
To a simpler place and time.
And I'll be with him
On that midnight train to Georgia,
I'd rather live in his world
Than live without him in mine.

This song is in the key of D flat major, with five flats in the key signature. This is not as difficult a key to play in as you might think – all the notes are flats except C and F. The tenor saxophones in the accompaniment are transposing instruments, so will be in the key of E flat major anyway.

Central to the accompaniment is a piano, which plays throughout, together with a bass guitar that plays a funky, syncopated line. These two instruments, together with the distinctive Hammond organ, provide the chord sequence that is persistently repeated, with some variation, throughout the song.

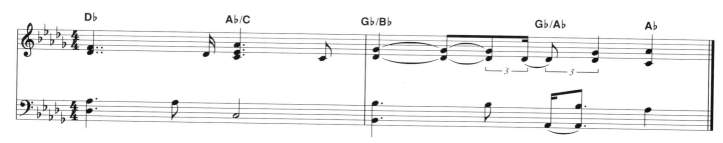

You can see that although only chords I, IV and V are used in this simple sequence, by using a descending step-wards bass line, the composer has created some interesting 'added' harmonies.

Listen to the 'horns' in the accompanying group (in pop and rock music, saxophones and brass instruments are often simply referred to as the horns). Note the way that they are used as punctuating instruments, as much for the rhythmic punches that they pull as for the harmonies that they play. Listen, too, to the strings, which play a combination of counter-melodies and an orchestral 'pad' – long sustained chords that help to pad out the musical texture and bind all of the musical elements together.

Notice that the drumbeat remains constant throughout the song. The drummer is playing a classic 1960s backbeat rhythm, with the second and fourth beats of the bar heavily emphasized by the drums, whilst the cymbal plays continuous quavers.

Listen carefully to the singing, particularly to the call and response textures; the free, almost improvisatory way that Gladys Knight sings her solo lines, and the tight, disciplined singing of the bvox group.

Listening tasks

◆ Using the words given to you on page 110, rewrite the lyrics for this song making clear the sections sung by the soloist and the bvox singers. Then annotate your lyrics score by indicating where the different accompanying instruments play and what they play.
◆ There is a score grid in the teacher's resource file to help you with this task.

ALL RIGHT NOW

Paul Rodgers and Andy Fraser

Throughout the 1960s, the American rock and roll and rhythm and blues styles were adopted and developed by musicians the world over. Other musical styles adopted elements of rock and new styles were created, as we have seen with reggae and soul. Throughout this time and throughout the development of these new styles, two things remained constant.

The first was the dominance of the twelve-bar blues chord sequence (or at least, chord sequences featuring the primary chords, I, IV and V) as the backbone of harmonic structures in popular music. The second was the continued use of the 'classic' guitar-bass guitar-keyboard-drums instrumentation as a central instrumentation for popular music. This is not to say that the instruments themselves did not develop during the 1960s, though. Advances in technology meant that electric guitars became more sophisticated, as did the amplifiers used to power them. Pedal effects, such as distortion, flange and overdrive, were also developed together with new, more colourful keyboard instruments, including the distinctive sound of the Hammond organ.

Heavy metal

During the 1960s a new style of rock music began to emerge that was heavily based in the harmonic tradition of rock and roll, but which also recognized the heavier and more colourful instrumental sounds that were developing. This style became known as **heavy rock** and then **heavy metal** (possibly because of the sharp 'edge' that this music had).

The British metal group Free was one of the earliest metal bands. Their first hit, *All Right Now*, was also their biggest hit, reaching number 2 in the charts in 1970. Since then, the song has become established as one of the most well-known metal anthems of all time.

Listen to CD 2, track 25, which features the opening of *All Right Now*.

> There she stood on the street,
> Smiling from her head to her feet.
> I said, 'Hey, what is this?'
> Now baby, maybe she's in need of a kiss.
>
> I said, 'Hey, what's your name baby?
> Maybe we can see things the same.
> Now don't you wait or hesitate.
> Let's move before they raise the parking rate.'
>
> All right now, baby,
> It's all right now.
> All right now, baby,
> It's all right now.

At the start of the song, we hear the four bar rhythm guitar/bass guitar riff that dominates the whole song:

Guitar styles

Notice several things about this riff. Firstly, it has a very pronounced rhythmic identity. The first two bars are characterized through the use of rests as much as they are characterized through the punchy chords that are played. Then, in bar 3, there is the faster syncopated rhythm.

Notice also that only two chords are used in this riff – the tonic chord of A (chord I) and the subdominant chord of D (chord IV). Finally, notice that throughout the riff, the bass guitar plays a pedal note, A, which is the tonic note for the whole song and is also the one note that is shared between the chords of A and D.

Generally, listen for the use of 'power chords' in the rhythm guitar line, where the root and the fifth of the chord are doubled or even tripled to give a thick, powerful sound. Listen also for the use of effects pedals.

Drum style

Now listen carefully to the rhythm track played by the drummer. The drum pattern is much heavier than the simple 'shuffle' rhythm of rock and roll, the 'one drop' rhythm of reggae, or the 'backbeat' rhythm of soul music.

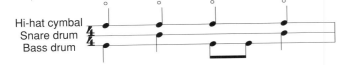

Notice that the bass drum plays on every beat of the bar and the hi-hat cymbal is often open.

Vocal style

As with the guitar chords, much of the vocal delivery is about sheer power (it has to be over such an accompaniment). Nevertheless, the vocal range is wide and the intonation and timbre of the solo singer (Paul Rodgers) is both accurate and well tuned.

Listening task

◆ Which other aspects of *All Right Now* identify it as being a song in the heavy metal/heavy rock style?

Image and message

Fashion and rebellion have always been (and always will be) important elements in pop music culture. Every style of pop music has had its associated clothing fashions and trends: the drain pipe trousers and suede shoes with rock and roll; the black leather and long hair with heavy metal; and the ripped clothing, spiked hair and safety pins that characterized the clothing of the punk rock movement. However, the punk fashions differed from the other two pop styles in that the image came *before* the music. It was Malcolm McLaren and Vivienne Westwood, boutiques owners in London's Kings Road, who 'invented' the punk look in the mid-1970s. McLaren then went on to form and manage the Sex Pistols, the first great punk band.

The punk movement

Much of the punk movement was about shock and scandal, about young people 'raging' against authority, boredom and the commercialism of much of the popular music scene at the time. Much of the punk music produced at this time was more about image and message than it was about producing serious, challenging music. However, some of the punk groups, such as The Jam and the Stranglers, progressed from the raw, protest music of bands like The Sex Pistols and produced a 'new wave' of music that, whilst encompassing many elements of the punk style, also had a progressive and innovative musical style.

Another new wave band was The Buzzcocks. Like Oasis, who would follow them 20 years later, this four-piece band hailed from Manchester. Listen to CD 2, track 26, which features a recording of The Buzzcocks' most successful song, *Ever Fallen in Love (With Someone You Shouldn't Have)?*

Listening tasks

◆ When you have listened to the extract from *Ever Fallen in Love (With Someone You Shouldn't Have)?* complete the table below by writing a brief comment about each listed aspect of The Buzzcocks' musical style.

Comment on the vocal style and range of the lead singer, Pete Shelley.	
Comment on the drumming, both in terms of the amount of drumming activity going on and the rhythms that the drummer uses.	
Comment on the harmonies. What do you notice about the chord progressions/changes, in particular?	
Comment on the range of guitar-playing techniques used in this song.	

You spurn my nat'ral e - mo - tions.
And if I start a com - mo - tion,

You make me feel like dirt
I run the risk of los -

- ing you, and I'm hurt.
and that's worse.

Ev - er

fall - en in love with some - one, ev - er fall - en in love, in love with some-

- one, ev - er fall - en in love, in love with some - one

- you shouldn't have fall - en in love with?

YOUR SONG
Elton John and Bernie Taupin

The ballad

The word **ballad** has been used to describe certain types of song since the medieval period of music history. In medieval times, a ballad was both a musical form and a type of poetry that told a story. More often than not, the story or the song had a strophic form (a number of verses that had the same form and metre) and a repeated chorus section.

The ballad is still a popular form of vocal composition, not least in pop and rock styles. In exactly the same manner as medieval ballads, contemporary pop ballads usually have a strophic format with repeated choruses. Most pop ballads have a slower tempo, fuller backing orchestrations and sophisticated harmonies. The slower tempo allows the singer to deliver the words (the story of the ballad) in a relaxed manner, giving meaning and expression to the story that is being told.

Listen to CD 2, track 27, which features a recording of Elton John singing his own ballad, *Your Song*.

It's a little bit funny, this feeling inside.
I'm not one of those who can easily hide.
I don't have much money but, boy, if I did,
I'd buy a big house where we both could live.

If I was a sculptor (but then again, no),
Or a man, who makes potions in a travelling show,
I know it's not much, but it's the best I can do.
My gift is my song and this one's for you.

And you can tell everybody,
This is your song.
It may be quite simple, but now that it's done,
I hope you don't mind, I hope you don't mind, that I put down in words
How wonderful life is, now you're in the world.

Like most ballads, this is a personal reflective song. The instrumentation at the start of the song reflects this introversion. Just a solo piano and solo acoustic guitar can be heard, backed by a sustaining string pad.

◆ Following the vocal/piano score for the opening four bars of this song, describe the music played by the acoustic guitar and the strings during the first verse.

◆ There are no drums playing in the extract that you hear on the CD. Is this an appropriate choice and how does the music manage to keep moving despite the slow tempo and the lack of percussion instruments?

Harmony

This song is in the key of E flat major. There are four beats in every bar, the harmonic rhythm (the rate at which the chords change) is generally two chords per bar. As you listen to the extract on the CD, follow through the chord pattern for the first verse.

You will notice a number of things about Elton John's choice of harmonies. Firstly, in the introduction, he manipulates the positioning of the chords so that the tonic note, E flat, is always at the bass of the chord. This gives a solid feel to the start of the song. Then, when the verse is underway, he manipulates the positioning of the chords so as to give a smooth, flowing bass line. He does this through the use of added chords and chromatic chords that are not part of the tonic key of E flat major.

Performance task

◆ There is a complete score of this song in the teacher's resource file. Use it to make your own arrangement of *Your Song*. Take up the challenge of arranging the song without using any percussion instruments, whilst keeping the slower tempo moving and with rhythmic interest.

A LITTLE RESPECT
Vince Clarke and Andy Bell

Pop!

In the same way that heavy metal used new guitar and amplifier technology to develop rock music in the 1960s and 1970s, the 1980s was the decade when computer technology really took off and reshaped the way in which popular music was composed and performed. In 1983, the introduction of the MIDI code – Musical Instrument Digital Interface – meant that musicians could use computers to record, store and even notate their music.

Erasure

One of the first and most successful of the 1980s 'synth groups' was Erasure. There were only two members of Erasure, Vince Clarke and Andy Bell, but their use of the new technology meant that, through the use of pre-sequenced tracks and a vast array of instrumental sounds that could be pre-programmed, their 'live' performances were large, dynamic and extravagant affairs.

Listen to CD 2, track 28, which features an extract from Erasure's 1988 hit single, *A Little Respect*.
As you can hear, the vocalist (Andy Bell) uses a range of almost two octaves.

Instrumental backing

The instrumental accompaniment for this song is sequenced and is based on a number of riff patterns that are constantly repeated throughout the song.

The first riff is heard on a piano/keyboard timbre and later doubled by a guitar timbre.

Towards the end of the first verse, we hear an even quaver riff that is played using a synthesizer timbre:

The drums, which have also been sequenced synthetically, have a similarly repetitive pattern.

The drum pattern takes a while to build up, but the basic drum pattern used throughout the song is:

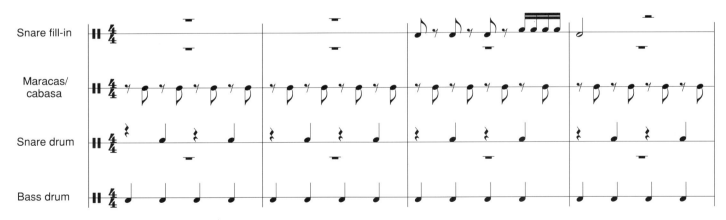

You will hear a number of other instrumental sounds in the accompaniment, including synth effects, bass synths and string timbres.

Listening tasks

◆ Study the vocal line printed on page 119. Comment on the word setting employed by the composers and also on the performance techniques of the vocalist in the different ranges of his voice.

◆ Describe how the instrumental accompaniment builds up during the first verse of the song. Pay attention to the pitched instrumental lines and the drum track.

Harmony

This song is in the key of C major. Listen to the opening of the first verse and, this time, concentrate on the harmonies that underpin the instrumental accompaniment.

C		**Csus4**	**C**	**Csus4**		**G**	**Gsus4**	**G**
I try to disco-		ver		a little something to make			me sweeter	
	Gsus4	**E**	**Esus4**	**E**	**Esus4**	**F**		**Fsus4** **F**
Oh baby refrain				from breaking my heart				
Fsus4 **C**		**Csus4**	**C**	**Csus4** **G**				**Gsus4** **G**
I'm so in love		with you		I'll be forev-		er blue,		
Gsus4		**F**			**Am**			
That you give me no		reason why you make me			work so hard,			
Gsus4	**G**			**C/G**		**G**		**C**
That you gimme no, that you gimme no,				that you gimme no, that you gimme no				soul.

You will notice that much use is made of the 'sus' chord. 'Sus' is an abbreviation of the word 'suspended'. In a 'sus' chord, a note from another chord is suspended, or sustained into the chord where it is not normally part of that chord. Here is an example.

In the chord of C there are three notes – C, E and G.

The note F is not part of the chord of C. However, if you played an F in the chord of C (instead of the E), you would have a 'Csus4' chord, where the fourth note (F) is suspended into the chord of C.

If, as the case with the first line of this song, the 'sus' chord is immediately followed by the regular version of the chord, it is said that the 'sus' chord has been resolved.

Look through the chord map given above and trace all the 'sus' chords and their resolutions in the first verse of this song.

Listening tasks

◆ What do you notice about the harmonic resources (choice of chords) used in this song?
◆ Which chords are primary chords in the key of C major?
◆ Which chords are secondary chords in the key of C major?
◆ Which chord is neither a primary nor a secondary chord in the key of C major?

If the *Prelude* from Charpentier's *Te Deum*, featured in the first project of *Heinemann GCSE Music*, is known best as the opening music to a television programme, then the music on CD 2, track 29 will need no introduction.

This is, of course, the fanfare that opens films made by Twentieth Century Fox. Even in this short six bar piece of music, there are a number of important ingredients that make the music work so well.

Firstly, there is the fact that the brass play in a homophonic texture, giving power and weight to the music and summoning the attention of the audience – 'the film is about to commence!' The same could be said about the unison strings and the drums at the very start. Secondly, the choice of brass instruments and the *forte* dynamic give further emphasis to the music. Lastly, note the use of the diminished chord formed by the last four notes in the string part and the chromatic shifts played by the brass during the fanfare itself. Next time you see a Twentieth Century Fox film and you hear the music, think about all of these musical elements that are bringing you to attention.

Cinema soundtracks

The story of the first 100 years of the cinema is shaped almost exactly by the twentieth century. During most of the first three decades of the century films were silent, without speech or a music soundtrack dubbed on to the film. There was music, played by live musicians in the 'pit' directly underneath the screen, and these musicians would synchronize their music to the action of the film as they watched the film themselves. Whilst this practice ended with the introduction of recorded soundtracks on to film, the principles that have governed the composition of film music ever since have remained the same, even as technology has advanced into the computer age.

Film music composers have to match their music not only to the mood or location of the action being shown on the film, they also have to synchronize the timing of their music to fit in exactly with the action. Composers plan this by working to a **cue-sheet**, where the action is written down to the exact fraction of a second. By working out exact rhythms and tempi, composers can ensure that their music fits perfectly.

Developing film music

The development of computer technology in the last quarter of the twentieth century made this task much easier. Through the use of SMPTE (a time code that works in conjunction with MIDI and digital video

imaging), composers and film directors can make synchronizations in the smallest detail. Of course, if the music is being composed and sequenced using synthesized instruments and MIDI, this is a natural development. But, even with 'live' music, performed by an orchestra for example, the soundtrack can be recorded digitally and this digital recording treated and manipulated in exactly the same way using SMPTE.

Common creative issues

Throughout the history of film music, from silent films with a pit orchestra to the hi-tech, SMPTE film scores of today, the same creative issues have faced composers. Their task is to reinforce, through music, the drama, philosophy and emotions portrayed or implied on the screen.

◆ Film music can create or reinforce the atmosphere of the film scene, whether this is an atmosphere of a place or of a relationship between two people.
◆ Film music can depict and reinforce an action that is taking place on the screen, like wind blowing or a blow being struck.
◆ Film music can be used in association with a particular character. For example, every time that a character appears, we hear the same motif, albeit modified to suit the time, place or the emotion at the time.
◆ Film music can 'set the scene'. For example, it can help to give the audience a feel for the country or era in which the film is set.

Using classic music

Sometimes directors choose not to commission new music for their films, but rather choose to re-use existing music that they feel matches the mood or events of their pictures. Choosing pop songs from the era in which the film is set is a particular favourite with directors, but art music from the Baroque, Classical and Romantic periods has also been used. Alternatively, contemporary composers have written music in a pastiche style, imitating aspects of different musical style.

In the rest of this project, we will look at five different film scores, which all take a different view of the art of composing or choosing music for a soundtrack. If you get a chance to see any of the films and put the music into context of a film, then do!

Brief Encounter

Not all film music is composed specifically for the film in which it features. Since the advent of the film soundtrack, directors and producers have used existing songs and compositions as theme and underscore music for their films where that music has been suited to the subject, the mood or the setting.

Such was the case with the 1945 black and white film *Brief Encounter*, based on the stage play by Noel Coward and directed by the great British film producer and director David Lean.

Background to the film

Brief Encounter, set in England during World War II, tells the story of a married woman who, whilst waiting at a station for a train, has a speck of soot blown into her eye. She is helped by a doctor and during the film the relationship between the woman and the doctor develops. Nothing actually happens between them and just before it might, they agree to part. In modern-day terms, the film might seem extremely tame, but it is the film's complete understatement and the fact that, in 1945, two married people might dare to even contemplate having an affair, that makes it all the more powerful.

Throughout the film, the woman and the doctor go about their business with characteristic reserve and decency, only once or twice does either of them show even the slightest sign of passion. But there is an undercurrent of passion and a desire to break free of their ordinary existences.

The music that Noel Coward and David Lean chose for the soundtrack to *Brief Encounter* is an archetypal Romantic composition, Sergei Rachmaninov's *Piano Concerto No. 2 in C minor*. The minor key turbulence and the dialogue between the piano and the orchestra is a perfect musical representation of the turbulence that underpins the lives of the two main characters in the film. At the same time, the broad sweep of Rachmaninov's melodies and orchestrations matches the power and the movement of the steam trains and the railway station that are a central feature of the film's setting.

Listen to CD 2, track 30, which features the start of the first movement from Rachmaninov's second piano concerto, and which also served as the opening theme music to the film *Brief Encounter*. The score that follows represents the melody line shared and played at various times by the orchestral strings.

Listening tasks

- Listen to the string melody that is represented by the score opposite. Which features of this melody and the way that it is performed identify it as being a work composed in the Romantic style?
- Go back through the score and, listening again to the extract on the CD, add details of dynamics, tempo, articulation and phrasing to the score as appropriate.
- Before the strings play this melodic line, the piano plays a solo passage. Describe the music played by the piano and suggest why Noel Coward and David Lean might have thought it to be a good musical representation of the doomed romantic relationship between the characters of the film.
- When the strings are playing the melody shown above, what is the piano playing? How does this music portray the turbulent relationship between the characters or the movement of the trains through the railway station that is the centre of the film's setting?

Hitchcock's and Herrmann's horror

The American composer Bernard Herrmann, who was born in New York in 1911, was without a doubt, one of the greatest composers of film underscore music in the twentieth century. During his career, he worked with many great and legendary directors, including Orson Welles, Martin Scorsese, and, most famously, Alfred Hitchcock. The partnership between Herrmann and Hitchcock included the classics *Vertigo*, *Cape Fear* and, most memorably of all, *Psycho* in 1960.

Composing an underscore for a film is a subtle and skilled task. Whilst most of the audience's attention is going to be focused on what they are viewing on the screen, the music that accompanies the images will reinforce the drama and the emotion in what they see.

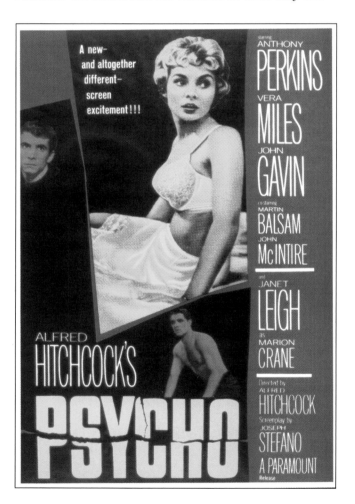

More than any composer before him, Herrmann seized on this and produced music of great drama and yet great subtlety. His music did not distract from the film image, rather it reinforced it.

Nowhere is this more apparent than in the score to *Psycho*. The story of the film is both gruesome and disturbing.

Background to the film

Marion Crane, an estate agent's secretary in Phoenix, Arizona, spends most of her lunch breaks with her lover, Sam Loomis. He owes money thanks to his father's debts and the alimony he must pay to his ex-wife. Desperate to escape the situation, Marion steals $40,000 from her boss and flees to meet up with Sam.

Tired after a long drive, the young woman stops at a motel run by the strange Norman Bates and his mother ...

So runs the opening of the film. What happens next is the gruesome part involving Marion Crane's bloody demise whilst taking a shower, possibly one of the most famous scenes in the history of the cinema.

Although the famous shower/murder scene lasts for barely 45 seconds, Hitchcock's aim was to keep the undercurrent of fear and suspense running throughout the film so that, even in the normal 'everyday' scenes, the audience would still experience feelings of foreboding. He would achieve this through his direction of shots and locations, and through Bernard Herrmann's underscore.

Listen to CD 2, track 31, which features part of Bernard Herrmann's music for *Psycho*. One particular feature of Herrmann's compositional technique is the way that he uses short musical motifs as reference points throughout the score and the film to identify individual characters emotions. Here are three of the main motifs/ideas that Herrmann uses in the extract.

The first idea uses a series of homophonic chords played in an aggressive, stabbing manner. There is no prize for guessing which event in the film this music refers to.

Notice three things about this 'stabbing' idea:

◆ The musical texture is very thick here, giving reinforcement to the heaviness of the chord.
◆ The chord is basically the chord of F major, but with the fourth (B flat) and the sharpened fifth (C sharp) added to make the sound extremely discordant.
◆ The offbeat rhythm used in bar 2 adds a further sense of disturbance to the motif.

The second idea is an ostinato motif.

There are two things to note:

◆ The regular quaver rhythm is akin to a heartbeat (and watching the film certainly does give the viewer a racing heartbeat!).
◆ The clash of B flat/C sharp, followed by the solo note of D, adds further disturbance to the musical texture.

The third idea features a high-pitched melodic motif.

Against the stabbing chords and ostinato figure, this idea had an almost neurotic quality emphasizing, perhaps, the disturbed state of Norman Bates' mind. Note the semitonal shift from A to A flat, giving a major/minor conflict to the music.

Listening tasks

◆ Listen to the music again, tracing Herrmann's use of these three motifs. What do you notice about the way in which the motifs work together to give an overall musical texture?
◆ Play through the first (chordal) motif, but as straight F major chords without the additional discordant notes. Does the chord have the same effect?

MUSIC FROM THE FILM
THE MAGNIFICENT SEVEN
Elmer Bernstein

The 1960 film *The Magnificent Seven*, starring, amongst others, Steve McQueen and Yul Brynner, is possibly the best-known western ever made. In actual fact, the film's storyline was not original; it was adapted from the cult Japanese film *The Seven Samurai* of 1954.

ⓘ Background to the film

In *The Magnificent Seven*, a group of seven hard and experienced gun fighters are picked to guard a Mexican village from a bandito gang, led by the ruthless Calvera, who comes every now and then to steal from the poor peasant folk. When they are hired, the seven go to the town and teach the villagers how to defend themselves. However, after the first fight the villagers realize that they have not rid themselves of Calvera yet and, soon after, much more bloodshed and fighting occur. Now the seven and the villagers are at odds with each other. Should the Magnificent Seven stay on? Or should the villagers fight for themselves and if so, at what cost? Most importantly – should the seven men abide by their own codes of honour and fight or should they leave?

Elmer Bernstein composed the music for the film *The Magnificent Seven*. The music was so successful and popular that it was nominated for an academy award (an Oscar).

There are two memorable ideas in Elmer Bernstein's theme tune for the film. The first is the distinctive homophonic, rhythmic accompanying figure:

The second is the 'big' tune that is played above the accompanying figure.

Listen to the arrangement of the theme from *The Magnificent Seven*, on CD 2, track 32. The extract falls into two distinct halves. In the first section, only the homophonic accompanying figure is heard. In the second half, the melody is added.

👂 Listening tasks

- In the first section, how is the homophonic/rhythmic idea used to build up the listener's sense of excitement and anticipation?
- In the second section, how does the main melody help to portray the image of the big, wide-open spaces of the American Wild West?
- In the second section, after the main tune has been played for the first time, it is heard again. How is it different second time around?
- In the second section, the homophonic/rhythmic idea continues playing. How is the orchestration for this section different?

Michael Nyman

The contemporary composer Michael Nyman has had a varied and diverse career in music. In the mid-1960s, he worked as a musicologist, editing works of Handel and Purcell. Later, he became interested in minimalism, in particular the work of Steve Reich, and started to compose his own music. He became involved in composing incidental music for the National Theatre in London and subsequently went on to compose music for dance productions. It was this interest in dramatic music that led him to composing music for films. His most famous film scores have been for films with the distinguished British film director Peter Greenaway, but he also had considerable success with his score for the Jane Campion film *The Piano*.

Nyman's musical style

In his film music, Michael Nyman shows an incredibly eclectic style. His personal compositional style has many different influences and flavours. As you will see with the extract from the Peter Greenaway film *The Draughtsman's Contract*, Nyman's early work and interest in Baroque music is an important influence, as is his interest in minimalism. Nyman is interested in contemporary popular music, too, and in 1998 he worked with Blur's Damon Albarn on a film score.

There are two other interesting points to note about Michael Nyman's work as a film composer. Firstly, he has his own ensemble, The Michael Nyman Band, for whom he frequently writes his scores. Secondly, in his working relationship with Peter Greenaway, it has been the case that Nyman has composed his music *before* Greenaway undertakes his filming, so the filming is cut and edited to music, rather than the music being edited to fit in with the filming, which is the usual practice.

Background to the film

Peter Greenaway's 1982 film *The Draughtsman's Contract*, with music by Michael Nyman, is set in the seventeenth century. The film tells the story of an aristocratic couple, Mr and Mrs Herbert, who are having some difficulties with their relationship. To give them both some time and space, Mr Herbert decides to take a short holiday by himself. While he is away, Mrs Herbert decides to commission a draughtsman to draw twelve landscape pictures of their estate as a surprise present for her husband's return. However, when the paintings are complete, Mr Herbert is discovered dead in the moat of his estate. How did he die? The answer lies within the twelve landscapes ...

The Draughtsman's Contract is a film that blends a number of styles. It is a mystery, it has elements of romance, there are moments of black comedy and much of the film is fantastical and surreal. The film is set in the seventeenth century, but made in the twentieth century. It is with this blend in mind that we come to Michael Nyman's music for the film.

Listen to CD 2, track 33, which features an excerpt from *The Draughtsman's Contract*, entitled *Chasing sheep is best left to shepherds*.

The Michael Nyman Band performs this recording. The instruments in the band include violins, viola and cello, piccolo, flute, trumpet, horn, trombone and piano – all standard orchestral instruments. Alongside these instruments are soprano, alto and baritone saxophones and a bass guitar – instruments you would normally expect to hear in popular and jazz styles. You may also hear a keyboard sound that is akin to the sound of a harpsichord, characteristic of Baroque music.

This score represents the opening of *Chasing sheep is best left to shepherds.*

Listen out for the following features of Michael Nyman's music:

◆ The way that the melody line is constructed from a short, repeated motif.
◆ The functional bass line, moving steadily by step in contrast to the melody line.
◆ The way that the saxophones are used in their high register to give a piercing sound, as opposed to the mellower sound that one more normally associates with a saxophone.

◆ Now listen to a second extract from *The Draughtsman's Contract*, entitled *An eye for optical theory*. The extract is on CD 2, track 34. This extract is founded on a jazzy, syncopated ground bass idea. When you have listened to this extract, go back to page 45 and revisit Purcell's *Sound the Trumpet*, which also uses a ground bass. How are the two pieces similar and how are they different in style?
◆ Which elements has Michael Nyman taken from the Baroque style and which elements have come from elsewhere?

Listening tasks

◆ When you have listened to *Chasing sheep is best left to shepherds*, go back to pages 61-3 of this book and compare the style of Michael Nyman's music with the style of Handel in *Zadok the Priest*. How are the two pieces similar and how are they different in style?
◆ Which elements has Michael Nyman taken from the Baroque style and which elements have come from elsewhere?

Advanced listening task

◆ In his early career, Michael Nyman studied and edited the works of Purcell and Handel. Later, he became very interested in minimalism. How have these interests of Nyman's manifested themselves in his personal compositional style, as represented here by the two extracts from *The Draughtsman's Contract*? In your answer, refer back to the music of Purcell, Handel and Phillip Glass that is featured in this book.

About the composer

Ennio Morricone was born in Rome in 1928. He first made his name as a composer of music for films in the early 1960s and in 1964, he shot to international recognition with his score for the Sergio Leone western, *A Fistful of Dollars*. Since then, he has composed over 350 film music scores, working with some of the greatest film directors in Hollywood and Italy. What makes Morricone's work particularly noteworthy is that he has composed music for many genres of film, including westerns, thrillers, science fiction and adventure movies.

Background to the film

In the early 1980s, Morricone composed the soundtrack for the film *The Mission*, which premiered in 1986. The film is set at the turn of the eighteenth century in the rainforests of South America. Two men, Father Gabriel (a Jesuit priest, played by Jeremy Iron) and Mendoza (a slave hunter, played by Robert De Niro) go into the forest for different reasons.

In the course of converting the Native South American Indians to Christianity, Father Gabriel meets Mendoza and converts him, too. Together they work in defence against the Portuguese, who are the new colonists of the rainforest. However, Mendoza is tempted by the colonists promise to allow the slave trade to flourish, and the two men are drawn into conflict against each other. Father Gabriel puts his trust in the power of prayer, whilst Mendoza relies on more physical strength to achieve his aims.

Influences

Morricone's music for the film draws on a whole host of musical influences, including Latin Church music (reflecting the Catholicism of Father Gabriel); Baroque instrumental textures and timbres (reflecting the time in which the film is set) and instrumental timbres idiomatic of the South American Indian music tradition, including panpipes and percussive sounds. Morricone also captures the magical, mystical mood of the rainforest through allusions to birdsong, water and warmth.

Two excerpts from the soundtrack to *The Mission* can be heard on CD 2 tracks 35 and 36. The first is a piece called *The Falls* and is scored for strings, harp, percussion and panpipes. A five-part arrangement of *The Falls* is given here for you to play. Part 1 is the part played on the recording by the panpipes. The other four parts are those played by the harp and strings. Note that no details of tempo, dynamics, phrasing and expression are given on the scores. You will need to listen carefully to the recording to help you decide on your choices for these musical parameters.

Part 1

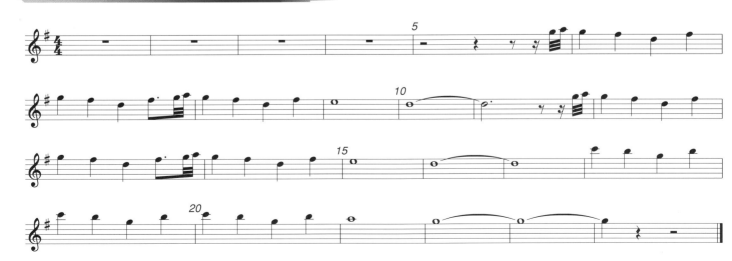

Part 2

Part 3

Part 4

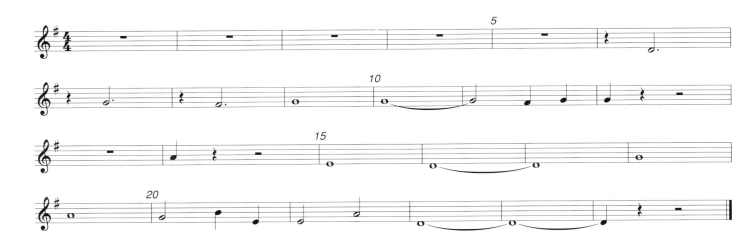

Part 5

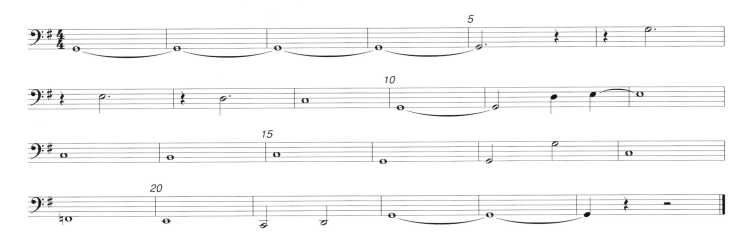

The second extract is a piece called *Gabriel's Oboe.*
Follow the score of the solo oboe part as you listen to
the recording on CD 2, track 36. Listen carefully for the
Baroque influences in the musical style, particularly the
harpsichord continuo, and the suspensions in the
harmonies played by the string parts.

Gabriel's oboe

Creating an impression

A new style of musical composition that developed in France during the early years of the twentieth century was **Impressionism**. In the same way that the French Impressionist painters used broad brush-strokes and blurred washes of colour to create an 'impression' of the scene that they were depicting, so the French Impressionist composers used broad washes of sound to depict mood or atmosphere in a piece of music. Often, this meant that melodies were flowing and built from colourful chromatic patterns, rather than being in clearly defined phrases. Rhythms were often fluid and complex, giving an impression of subtle movement rather than driving the music forward.

Claude Debussy is the best-known French Impressionist composer. One of his most famous works is *Prélude á L'Aprés Midi D'un Faune*.

Listen to CD 2, track 37, which features a recording of Debussy's impressionistic piano piece *La fille aux cheveux de lin*. Follow this score as you listen.

La fille aux cheveux de lin is one of Debussy's *First Book of Twelve Preludes for Piano*. The title means 'the girl with the flaxen hair' and was inspired by a poem by the poet Leconte de Lisle. The poem asks and answers the question:

> *Who is it sitting in the flowering Lucerne?*
> *Why, it is the girl with the flaxen hair, the*
> *beautiful girl with the cherry-red lips …*

In his piano piece, Debussy creates a musical impression of this beautiful young girl sitting peacefully on the grass in the summer sunshine. As you can see, Debussy's original music has a key signature of six flats.

For the performance tasks that follow, *La fille aux cheveux de lin* has been transposed down a semitone.

Performance tasks

For this task, *La fille aux cheveux de lin* has been arranged into five parts – four treble parts and one bass part. All parts are at concert pitch. If any of your instruments are transposing instruments, then you will need to transpose them as appropriate. Alternatively, this arrangement is given as a MIDI file on the *Heinemann GCSE Music CD-ROM*, so you could transpose the parts using MIDI.

Part 1

Part 2

Part 3

Part 4

Part 5

◆ Play through these opening seven bars of *La fille aux cheveux de lin* in your group. Refer to Debussy's original piano score for details of dynamics, phrasing and expression.

◆ When you have done this, go on to bars 8–16 and continue with the arrangement. Allocate the notes in the piano score by continuing in the same style and the same pitch ranges as has been done for you in bars 1–7. Remember that the music has been transposed down a semitone.

◆ An alternative method of completing this task would be to use the MIDI file provided on the *Heinemann GCSE Music CD-ROM*.

Listening tasks

When you have completed the performance tasks (and perhaps made a recording of your own arrangements and performances), go back to the recording on CD 2, track 37. Follow the piano score as you listen and answer the following questions.

◆ Study the top line in bars 1–2. What do you notice about the notes that make up this line? What happens if you play them all together at the same time?

◆ What do you notice about the movement (direction) of the melody and the chords in bars 2 and 3?

◆ What does the instruction 'Très calme et doucement expressif' mean? From an impressionistic point of view, how important and meaningful is this instruction?

◆ What do you notice about the chords in bars 8 and 9?

◆ What do you notice about the rhythm and tempo in this piece, from an impressionistic point of view?

LITTLE PIANO PIECE NO. 6, OP. 19

Arnold Schoenberg (1874–1951)

A personal expression

At much the same time as the French composer Debussy was composing in the Impressionist style, the Austrian composer Arnold Schoenberg was composing music in what became known as the Expressionist style. Like Impressionism in music, the music **Expressionist** style also had a parallel in the visual arts. You may know the painting called *The Scream*, which is a famous Expressionist work.

In his Expressionist compositions, Schoenberg believed that he should be free to express all manner of human mood and emotion through his music without any restriction on form, structure, tonality or any musical convention. Consequently, his Expressionist compositions are 'free' in the extreme. More importantly, the music was **atonal** – the music was not set in or based around any particular key or tonal centre. What was more important to Schoenberg was the emotional effect that was created by the combination of different pitches, either as a chord or in a melody.

Study this score of Schoenberg's *Little Piano Piece No. 6, Op. 19* and listen to the recording of the piece on CD 2, track 38.

You will see (and hear) that this is an atonal composition. There are no clues about which note or chord is the conventional tonic of this piece. Notice the way that Schoenberg does not allow his expression to be constrained by bar lines or beats within the bar – rhythm is extremely fluid and flexible. Also notice the great range of expression marks and dynamics used by Schoenberg in this Expressionist piece.

Having said all of this, you will notice that Schoenberg does have some reference points within the piece – there are two or three musical motifs that keep occurring throughout.

Performance tasks

◆ If you are a pianist or keyboard player, try giving your own performance of this piano piece by Schoenberg. The actual notes themselves may not be the most challenging aspect of the music, assuming that your hands can span the wide ranges of some of the chords! Do your best to play the rhythms and the dynamics as accurately as possible.

◆ Thinking back to the arrangement of *Debussy's La fille aux cheveux de lin* on pages 136–8, make your own arrangement of Schoenberg's piano piece for the same group of instruments. You could then perform both pieces side-by-side in a concert to illustrate two contrasting approaches to composition at the start of the twentieth century.

From atonal to serial

After his experiments with atonal Expressionist music, Schoenberg developed a new composition technique that, whilst certainly not based on the major/minor key system, used a type of scale as the basis of form and structure in a piece of music. This technique became known as the **twelve-tone** or **serial** composition technique.

Every piece of twelve-tone music is based on a scale that is devised especially for that piece of music. The principle that governs the construction of that scale is that the scale must contain twelve different notes – the twelve different notes to be found within an octave on the keyboard – and that each note can be used only once.

So, in a tone row, a composer must use all of the twelve pitches within an octave:

Each of these notes can only be used once. The notes can be in any order, so a tone row could look like this:

Once the tone row has been devised, it is possible to derive a large number of variations from within it. It can be played backwards (retrograde), it can be played with the intervals upside-down (inversion), and it can be played with the intervals upside-down *and* backwards (retrograde inversion). Each one of these can be transposed to start on any one of the twelve notes within the octave.

The first piece that Schoenberg composed using a tone row is the *Waltz* from *Piano Pieces Op. 23*.

Follow through the score for this piece as you listen to the recording on CD 2, track 39.

The tone row can be heard clearly, played in the piano right hand in bars 1–4. Here is the tone row in 'closed' notation:

Listening tasks

◆ Compare the waltz style of Schoenberg with that of Johann Strauss, as featured on pages 82–3. Apart from the fact that the Strauss composition is tonal and the Schoenberg is serial, what are the other differences in musical style between the two compositions?

An infernal noise

A third style of musical composition from the early years of the twentieth century can be found in the orchestral works of the Russian composer Igor Stravinsky. Stravinsky was the son of a singer in the St Petersburg Opera, where he learnt a great deal simply by listening to the great orchestra of the opera house. After studying the piano, he became a composition pupil of the great Russian composer Rimsky-Korsakov. As well as teaching Stravinsky the all-important basic techniques of harmony and counterpoint, Rimsky-Korsakov's own orchestral works are extremely colourful, making excellent use of the whole kaleidoscope of orchestral colours and effects. You may well know his famous piece *Flight of the Bumblebee*, with an extraordinarily effective (and difficult) part for the solo flute.

Stravinsky clearly learnt a great deal about orchestration from his teacher and in his three major orchestral scores written for the ballet – *The Firebird*, *Petrouchka* and *The Rite of Spring* – he produced music that used some of the largest, most colourful and most flamboyant orchestrations ever heard.

ⓘ Background to The Firebird

The Firebird is an old Russian fairytale that tells of the story of the good Prince Ivan, who, with the aid of a magic feather given to him by the mystic Firebird, sets out to rescue a group of beautiful princesses from the clutches of the wicked King Kastchei. At one point in the ballet, King Kastchei attempts to hypnotize and imprison Prince Ivan but, in the nick of time, the Firebird makes a dramatic appearance and forces Kastchei and his evil band of followers to dance an 'infernal dance' until they all fall down exhausted.

This *Infernal Dance* is one of the most dramatic parts of the ballet and the music that Stravinsky composed for it is certainly colourful and descriptive. One glance at Stravinsky's score shows the huge range of instruments and instrumental effects, not to mention an extreme range of dynamics, which he uses to paint the scene of King Kastchei dancing himself into the ground.

Performance task

◆ A performance of Stravinsky's *Infernal Dance* can be heard on CD 2, track 40. You could try your own performance, using the seven-part arrangement that follows. Listen carefully to the recording and edit your score accordingly. You will have to transpose parts where appropriate.

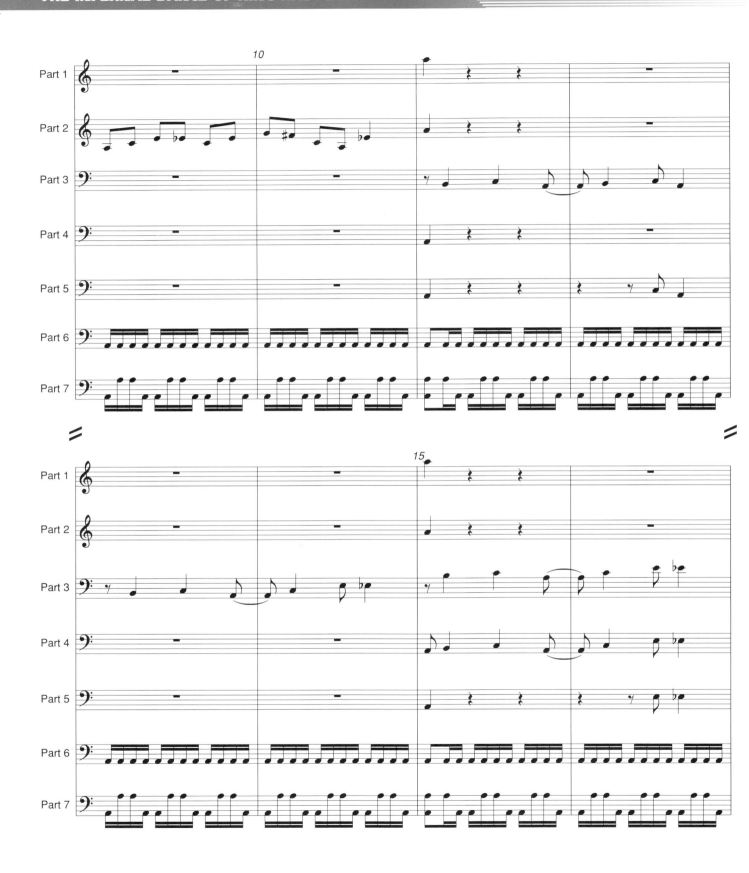

LIGHTNING FROM SONGS FROM LIQUID DAYS

Philip Glass

One of the most important compositional styles in Western art music since 1960 has been **minimalism**. The principles underpinning minimalist compositions are not unlike the structures that govern Indonesian Gamelan music – that the music is constructed from small motifs or units that are constantly repeated, only changing in progressively small details. The musical effect is similar to the visual effect created by a kaleidoscope, where the constantly turning image changes in small stages.

Two of the best-known composers of minimalist music are the Americans Steve Reich (b. 1936) and Philip Glass (b. 1937). Both composers have produced music for the stage, the concert hall and for film and video.

Listen to CD 2, track 41, which features the opening of Philip Glass's song *Lightning*, with words by Suzanne Vega and orchestral/choral arrangement by Jeremy Marchant.

*Lightning struck a while ago, blazing much
    too fast.
But it gave rain of waiting time,
And it will surely pass.
Blow over …
And it's happening so quickly as I feel the
    flaming time.
And I grope about the embers to relieve my
    stormy mind.
Blow over, blow over …*

This song is built on a number of ideas that are repeated and developed minimalistically during the course of the piece. The opening idea (A) is a simple repeated quaver rhythm featuring octave bass leaps.

The second idea puts syncopated chords over this bass line.

Later, both the bass line and the syncopated chords are developed.

A different type of syncopated chord pattern is used later in the song.

D

Finally, at some points, a quaver-triplet figuration is used.

E

Listening tasks

Listen to the recording of *Lightning*, which is featured on CD 2, track 41, and answer the following questions.

◆ Which instrument plays idea **A**?
◆ How are the syncopated chords of idea **B** performed?
◆ Which instrument joins the ensemble for idea **C**?

◆ Describe the accompaniment given when the words 'Lightning struck ...' are first sung.
◆ How does the music build up for the words 'Blow over ...' the first time?
◆ What happens in the accompaniment after the words 'Blow over ...' are first sung?
◆ What happens in the accompaniment after the words 'Blow over ...' are sung for the second time?

ANGEL
James MacMillan

Less is more

And finally, the last piece of music to be featured in this book is the simplest and yet, in many ways, one of the most thought provoking pieces that we have analysed. At the end of the twentieth century, composers were taking a **total** approach to music composition, regarding the music as a completely multi-dimensional art. This approach can be seen in *Angel*, a piano piece from 1993, by the Scottish composer James MacMillan, who was born in 1959. The pitches of the notes are

important; you will be able to see a number of motifs in the piece, including the interval of a perfect fifth, which recurs from time to time. However, other elements, such as volume, articulation, duration and silence are just as important. On the score, James MacMillan suggests that 'the pause on each note should last between six and ten seconds, the length of each note being varied as the piece progresses'. Listen to CD 2, track 42.

Try performing *Angel* by yourself. Even if you find it relatively easy to play technically, in terms of notes of the keyboard, you will enjoy the challenge of interpreting MacMillan's work.

Track 1: *Prelude* from *Te Deum* by Charpentier. Used by permission of EMI Records.

Track 2: *Georgy Girl* by Tom Springfield and Jim Dale. Used by permission of EMI Records.

Track 3: *Gavotte* from *Orchestral Suite No. 1 in C major* by J.S. Bach. Used by permission of HNH International Ltd.

Track 4: *Symphony No. 29, K201, 1st movement* by Mozart. Used by permission of HNH International.

Track 5: *Study for Clarinet No. 23.* Written and performed by Chris Allen. Used by kind permission of Chris Allen.

Track 6: *Scale Study for Violin* by Mark Phillips, performed by Ian Smith. Used by kind permission of Mark Phillips.

Track 7: *Power to All Our Friends* by Doug Flett and Guy Fletcher. Used by permission of EMI Records.

Track 8: *Queen of the Night's Aria* from *The Magic Flute* by Mozart, performed by James Levine. Licensed courtesy of BMG Entertainment.

Track 9: *Ain't Misbehavin'* by Fats Waller. Licensed courtesy of BMG Entertainment.

Track 10: *All Out of Luck* by Selma, Thorvaldur B Thorvaldur, Sveinbjorn I Baldvinsson. Used by kind permission of NCB.

Track 11: *It's a Sin* by Neil Tennant and Chris Lowe. Used by permission of EMI Records.

Track 12: *Sinfonia Concertante, K297b, 3rd movement* by Mozart. Used by permission of EMI Records.

Track 13: *Symphony No. 6, 1st movement* by Beethoven. Used by permission of HNH International Ltd.

Track 14: *Reach* by Cathy Dennis and Andrew Todd. Courtesy of Polydor. Licensed by kind permission from the Universal Film and TV Licensing Department.

Track 15: *Variations on a Theme by Haydn* by Brahms. Used by permission of HNH International Ltd.

Track 16: *La Mourisque* from *Danserye* by Susato. Courtesy of Decca. Licensed by kind permission from the Universal Film and TV Licensing Department.

Track 17: *Brandenburg Concerto No. 2 in F major, 1st movement* by J.S. Bach. Used by permission of HNH International Ltd.

Track 18: *Sound the Trumpet: Come, Ye Sons of Art, Away* by Henry Purcell. Performed by John Eliot Gardiner/ Monteverdi Choir and Orchestra (p) 1976 Erato Classics SNC, Warner Classics/Warner Strategic Marketing UK.

Track 19: *Piano Concerto No. 24 in C major, K491, 3rd movement* by Mozart. Used by permission of HNH International Ltd.

Track 20: *Symphony No. 103, 4th movement* by Haydn. Courtesy of Deutsche Grammophon. Licensed by kind permission from the Universal Film and TV Licensing Department.

Track 21: *Prelude in C minor* by Chopin. Used by permission of HNH International Ltd.

Track 22: *Romeo and Juliet* by Tchaikovsky, performed by Charles Munch. Licensed courtesy of BMG Entertainment.

Track 23: *Don't Stop the Carnival* by Sonny Rollins. Licensed courtesy of BMG Entertainment.

Track 24: *St Thomas* by Sonny Rollins. Licensed courtesy of BMG Entertainment.

Track 25 and 26: *Le Carnaval Romain* by Berlioz. Courtesy of Phillips. Licensed by kind permission from the Universal Film and TV Licensing Department.

Track 27: *Zadok the Priest* by Handel. Performed by John Eliot Gardiner/Monteverdi Choir and Orchestra (p) 1978 Erato Classics SNC, Warner Classics/Warner Strategic Marketing UK.

Track 28: *Crown Imperial* by William Walton. Chandos, TRCD 2. Used with permission from Chandos Records.

Track 29: *Yom Holedet (Happy Birthday)* by Eden. Used with permission of IMP Records, Israel.

Track 30: *Wedding March* from *A Midsummer Night's Dream* by Mendelssohn. Courtesy of Deutsche Grammophon. Licensed by kind permission from the Universal Film and TV Licensing Department.

Track 31: *March* from *Music for the Funeral of Queen Mary* by Henry Purcell. Licensed courtesy of BMG Entertainment.

Track 32: *Canzona* from *Music for the Funeral of Queen Mary* by Henry Purcell. Licensed courtesy of BMG Entertainment.

Track 1: *Salterello* by anon. Used by permission of EMI Records.

Track 2: *Symphony No. 4, 4th movement* by Mendelssohn. Used by permission of EMI Records.

Track 3: *Bourée* from *Orchestral Suite No. 2* by J.S. Bach. Used by permission of HNH International Ltd.

Track 4: *Symphony No. 41, 3rd movement* by Mozart. Used by permission of HNH International Ltd.

Track 5: *Morning Papers* by Johann Strauss. Used by permission of EMI Records.

Track 6: *Dick's Maggots.* Written and performed by Roger Nicholls. Used by kind permission of Roger Nicholls.

Track 7: *The Charleston/Five Foot Two* by Cecil Mack and Jimmy Johnson, perf. by BYJO. Used by kind permission.

Track 8: *Rock Around the Clock* by Max C. Freedman and Jimmy De Knight. Used by kind permission of Charly Licensing APS.

Track 9: *Stayin' Alive* by The Bee Gees. Courtesy of Polydor. Licensed by kind permission from the Universal Film and TV Licensing Department.

Track 10: *Rewind* performed by Craig David. Used by kind permission of Wildstar Records Ltd.

Track 11: *Raag Bhoplal* by Irshad Khan. Used by permission of HNH International Ltd.

Track 12: *Raag Bilaskhani Todi* by Anindo Chatterjee. Used by permission of Nimbus Records.

Track 13: *Rahaye, Rahaye* by The Safri Boys. Licensed courtesy of BMG Entertainment.

Track 14: *Nukhe Chakee Javana* by Achanak. Used by permission of Nachural Records.

Track 15: *Aag* by CID (Commercial Indian Dance). Licensed courtesy of BMG Entertainment.

Track 16: *Bamboleo* by Baliardo, Bouchikhi and Reyes. Used by kind permission of Sonido, Inc.

Track 17: *Keybar ding III: oncang-oncangan* by Colin McPhee. Taken from *The Roots of Gamelan*, WA 2001. Used by permission of Arbiter/World Arbiter Records; www.arbiterrecords.com

Track 18: *The Israelites* by Desmond Dekker and the Aces. Used by kind permission of Sanctuary Records Group.

Track 19: *Liph'Iqiniso* by Ladysmith Black Mambazo. Courtesy of Gallo Music International, a division of Gallo Africa Limited.

Track 20: *Ngoma Yekwedu* is used by permission of aNOnym reCOrds. © (p) 2002 aNOnym reCOrds. All Rights Reserved. aNOnym reCOrds, 460 Pennsylvania Ave., San Francisco, CA 94107 USA. anonymousweb.com © Chimurenga Music Company. All Rights Reserved.

Track 21: *The Voice* by Brendan Graham. (p) by Acorn Music. Used by permission of Brendan Graham and Peermusic.

Track 22: *March* from *English Folk Song Suite* by Vaughan Williams. Courtesy of Decca. Licensed by kind permission from the Universal Film and TV Licensing Department.

Track 23: *Blue Suede Shoes* by Carl Perkins. Used by kind permission of Charly Licensing APS.

Track 24: *Midnight Train to Georgia* by Jim Weatherley. Licensed courtesy of BMG Entertainment.

Track 25: *All Right Now* by Paul Rodgers and Andy Fraser. Courtesy of Island Ltd. Licensed by kind permission from the Universal Film and TV Licensing Department.

Track 26: *Ever Fallen in Love* by The Buzzcocks. Used by permission of EMI Records.

Tracks 27: *Your Song* by Elton John and Bernie Taupin. Courtesy of Mercury Ltd. Licensed by kind permission from the Universal Film and TV Licensing Department.

Track 28: *A Little Respect* by Erasure. Used by permission of Mute Records.

Track 29: Twentieth Century Fox Opening Fanfare by Alfred Newman. Performed by London Symphony Orchestra. Licensed courtesy of BMG Entertainment.

Track 30: *Piano Concerto No. 2 in C minor, 1st movement* by Rachmaninov. Courtesy of Decca. Licensed by kind permission from the Universal Film and TV Licensing Department.

Track 31: Theme music from *Psycho*, FILMXCD 320, 1999, The City of Prague Philharmonic Orchestra conducted by Paul Bateman © Silva Screen Records Ltd.

Track 32: Theme music from *The Magnificent Seven* by Elmer Bernstein. Used by kind permission of MGM.

Track 33: *Chasing Sheep is best left to Shepherds* from *The Draughtsman's Contract* by Michael Nyman. Courtesy of Decca. Licensed by kind permission from the Universal Film and TV Licensing Department.

Track 34: *An Eye for Optical Theory* from *The Draughtsman's Contract* by Michael Nyman. Courtesy of Decca. Licensed by kind permission from the Universal Film and TV Licensing Department.

Track 35: *The Falls* from *The Mission* by Ennio Morricone. Used by kind permission of Virgin Records Limited.

Track 36: *Gabriel's Oboe* from *The Mission* by Ennio Morricone. Used by kind permission of Virgin Records Limited.

Track 37: *La fille aux cheveux de lin* by Debussy. Used by permission of HNH International Ltd.

Track 38: *Little Piano Piece No. 6, Op. 19* by Schoenberg. Used by permission of HNH International Ltd.

Track 39: *Waltz* from *Piano Pieces Op. 23* by Schoenberg. Used by permission of HNH International Ltd.

Track 40: *Infernal Dance* from *The Firebird* by Stravinsky. Used by permission of Hungaroton Records, Kft.

Track 41: *Lightning* from *Songs from Liquid Days* by Philip Glass, SILKCD 6023, 2000, The Crouch End Festival Chorus/The National Sinfonia conducted by David Temple © Silva Screen Records Ltd.

Track 42: *Angel* by James MacMillan, performed by Lynsey Brown. Used by kind permission.